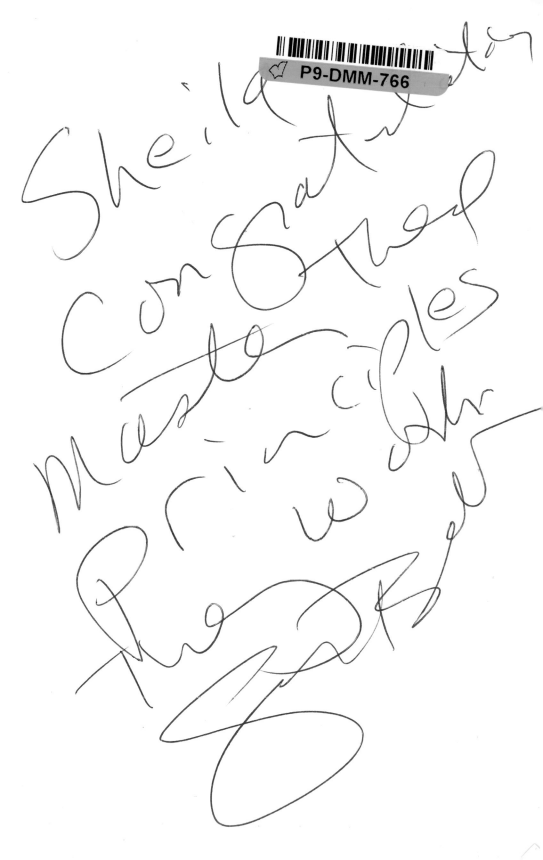

JOHN TSCHOHL
EMPOWERMENT

a Way of Life

1st edition

John Tschohl

BEST SELLERS PUBLISHING
Minneapolis, Minnesota USA

Published by Best Sellers Publishing, Minneapolis, Minnesota.

No part of this book may be used or reproduced in any manner or form without
written permission from the publisher except in the case of brief quotations in articles
and reviews. For information, address Best Sellers Publishing, 9201 East Bloomington
Freeway, Minneapolis, Minnesota 55420, USA. Phone: (952) 888-7672 /
Fax: (952) 884-8901, E-mail: bsp@bestsellerspublishing.com,
Web: www.BestSellersPublishing.com.

Library of Congress Cataloging-in-Publication Data:
Tschohl, John.
Empowerment: A Way of Life
p.   cm.
Includes index.
ISBN 13: 978-0-98263690-9
ISBN 10: 0-98263690-3
1. Customer Service   I. Title
HF54 15.5T83   2010   95-080722
658.8'12—de20   CIP

Printed in the United States of America.

Table of Contents

Acknowledgement

First and foremost I would like to thank my wife, Pat. She has tolerated my obsession with customer service for more than 30 years. For my children, Christina, a missionary in China, and Matthew, an entrepreneur in Colorado, my passion has been a mixed blessing. I'm proud to say that the upside is that they have learned to demand great service.

Sam Naheim and David Hahn were instrumental with their input in this book. Lauri Flaquer pushed me to make the book stronger and encouraged me to add more stories that demonstrate the power of empowerment.

Hannah Dorland and Jacob Yanish supported me through this process and offered valuable insights. My staff at Service Quality Institute help me on a daily basis in ways too numerous to mention. I appreciate your loyalty.

Finally, I would like to thank my grandson, William. You have given me reason to continue my commitment to customer service. I hope my efforts will culminate in universal empowerment and that you will be one of millions of overhappy customers.

Foreword

Great companies see customers as assets and opportunities, not problems and costs. Every great company has three essential elements:

Model:	Unique, differentiated, and value added
Culture:	Persuasive, infectious, and consistent with the model
Execution:	Fanatical and constantly improving

John's book is about empowering your team to fanatically execute your model. WHAT COULD BE MORE IMPORTANT than creating a model and culture that empowers your team and rewards initiative?

Thank you John, for giving us even
more tools to create
FANS NOT CUSTOMERS.

Vernon W. Hill, II
Founder, Commerce Bank
Co-Founder, Metro Bank, London

Introduction

In this book you will learn effective ways to use **Empowerment** to ramp up your career, to build your business, and to take your corporation to the top. Before we launch in, I'd like to tell you a story about **Empowerment** from my personal experience.

The story starts in a little bodega (grocery store) in the San Isidro District of Lima, Peru in 1942. The store, which is named E Wong, is owned by Chinese immigrants, Erasmo and Angela Wong. Dedicated and hard working, they focus on providing the best possible service to their customers. As you can imagine, hours are long and there's never a shortage of work. Life revolves around the little store. The children learn the business from the ground up by helping out after school and on weekends. They are successful. You can tell because the store gets busier and busier. After a few years, E Wong is so crowded that they need more space. They expand and hire a few employees.

Assuming the increased shopping area and additional staff would make the store less crowded, the Wongs are surprised when the expansion has little effect. Soon they expand again and hire more employees. Their focus remains on customer service, and when they have 25 employees they purchase my Feelings Customer Service Program. That was over 20 years ago.

At my first public seminar in Lima, about 15 years ago, the entire Wong family attended. During that presentation I asked, *"Who is the most customer service driven firm in Peru?"* Over two thirds of the audience said *"Wong"*. (About 99 percent of the time in my seminars the audience has trouble coming up with any answers at all to that question.)

Every few years the Wong family would have me train their entire work force. My sessions were big events. I would train between 1,000 to 2,800 employees at a time. In order to accommodate groups of this size, they had to erect an auditorium for my presentations. It would have been impossible for a staff member not to understand the level of importance that the Wongs placed on my message. The heaviest focus was always on **Empowerment**. I would teach all their employees to bend the rules, in favor of the customer, and to use **Empowerment** every day. I would come up with crazy things -- sure to surprise customers -- such as, if a child drops his ice cream cone, replacing it for free and delivering groceries for an elderly person who has trouble carrying them.

Many of their employees were very young. Invariably one person would raise a hand and say, *"Mr. Tschohl, if we did this we'd be fired."* The entire audience would erupt with applause and stamp their feet in agreement. Each time, I would ask Eduardo Wong, who would sit in the back of the auditorium, to come up and reinforce my message. I would say, with him standing on stage right beside me, that the Wong family would not miss a meal if employees spent company money taking care of customers.

In 2005, E. Wong changed its company name to The Wong Group to better reflect the business. It had become the largest supermarket and retailer in Peru. In the city of Lima, with about 9 million inhabitants in a country of approximately 29 million people, the Wongs built a reputation for service. The last time I worked with them they had over 10,000 employees, 34 stores and an internationally recognized online presence. Sales were approximately $1.1 billion dollars. Wong's had a 63 percent market share, and NO company had a better reputation for caring for its employees.

On December 17, 2007 the Wong Group sold the company for approximately $900 million to Cencosud, a Chilean company. To date there has been a sharp decline in stock value, and the future of Peru's former king of supermarkets isn't looking bright.

The problem is the new firm apparently doesn't know what it bought. The focus on **Empowerment**, customer service and caring for employees has eroded. The Wong Group remains number one although it's rapidly losing market share to its competitor, Supermercados Peruanos.

Once management takes its eyes off the service strategy, that company loses sight of its service to customers. Along with it goes market share and revenue and, unfortunately, they are almost impossible to recover. In two short years Wongs' brand and market share have been gutted. The Wong Group was an example of a firm that focused on driving an empowered work-force to offer superior service. It understood the power of **Empowerment** and its economic impact at Wong. Its caring for customers and employees fueled revenue. The Wong family still understands the power of customer service. It's new mall, Plaza Norte, is the largest and most luxurious in Peru and will be built on a solid brand formed on service strategy.

On a recent trip to Peru, I met up with Eduardo Wong again, and he quickly repeated the words I had taught thousands of Wong's employees. I chuckled as I heard my exact phrase pop out his mouth: ***"Empowerment is having millions and millions and millions and millions of overhappy customers."***

The Wong Group story is not an isolated incident; I have many other examples of **Empowerment** – all leading to success. Still the Wongs are one of the best examples because of their time in business and the abundance of well-documented information on how that success was achieved.

Read on to learn how Empowerment: A Way of Life can fuel your success...

The Scary Facts 1

I don't believe you can be a service leader without **Empowerment**. I've never met a CEO anywhere in the world who disagreed with my concept of **Empowerment**, which is to get employees to make a decision, on the spot, in favor of a customer. All CEO's believe their employees are empowered. The reality is that it doesn't happen, and empowered employees just don't exist.

Even the most customer-driven companies like Nordstrom, TD Bank, and Dell have huge problems. They can't get an employee to make an empowered decision. About 90 percent of all empowered decisions will cost less than $50.00. The Ritz Carlton has a $2,000 ceiling that an employee can spend on the spot. A typical guest spends thousands on a stay at the Ritz, so the amount makes sense. Maybe at your company the amount should be $200 or $500. Getting an employee to make a $25 - $50 decision in favor of the customer is like asking for two miracles at the same time. The single biggest reason employees won't make an empowered decision is because they fear getting fired. If it's between getting fired or losing the customer, it's an easy choice.

Empowerment is a myth, while all CEO's think that their employees are empowered, the reality is they are afraid to make even the smallest decisions.

11

"Half the money we spend on advertising is wasted, and the problem is we do not know which half."
Lord Leverhulme
British, Philanthropist, Founder of Unilever

The best way to test this is to try to get employees at companies where you do business to bend the rules. Ask them, *"What would happen if you made an empowered decision?"* They'll usually laugh and say, *"What's Empowerment? Are you kidding?"* And when you push them further, 95 percent of the time employees will say they'll get fired.

That same perception is true in your organization, contrary to your beliefs. If you don't make an empowered decision, the customer will probably leave and not return. Very few customers complain or push the problem up the chain of command. They just walk. The fear that some executives have is that an employee might give away too much. I suspect that half of your marketing money is wasted. The problem is that nobody knows which half. When you put an ad in the newspaper, on radio or TV, very few people even pay attention. The truth is they've come to distrust advertising. Of those who are exposed to the ad, even fewer respond. Of those who do respond, you have no idea who they are or what motivated them to buy. Most marketing people claim to have these answers, but in reality they don't.

You have a live customer in your hands and something goes wrong. Your employee could easily solve this problem with **Empowerment** and maybe a small amount of money. You have targeted marketing money. Isn't it better to use your marketing money to keep that customer happy? What's the worst thing that can happen?

An employee might give away too much. Now you have an overhappy customer. If you have overhappy customers you'll own the market and you'll have more money than you ever dreamed of.

Here's an excellent example of lack of Empowerment

I was checking in for my Minneapolis/St Paul to El Salvador flight. I had no idea that, when Continental Airlines discontinued its alliance with Sky Partners, it would affect my trip. On Delta, I was a Platinum Elite traveler, which was the highest volume status at that time.

The employee at the Continental First Class check-in counter said they no longer honored the baggage allowances of Delta. I had three bags; two weighed 55 pounds, and the third weighed 45 pounds. Previously I could fly with three bags, each weighing 70 pounds.

The employee said I had to pay overweight fees for two bags and pay extra for the third bag. I had no idea of the change in baggage allowances.

What she should have said is, *"Mr. Tschohl, Continental Airlines has changed its alliance with Delta. We would love to see you fly more with us, so I'm going to waive the fees and hope we'll be seeing more of you here at Continental Airlines."* I'm probably one of the top 1 percent of flyers. If I'm not their targeted customer, I don't know who is.

I took all the excess weight out of the two bags and put it in my carry-on baggage. They charged me for the third bag, and I was a very unhappy customer. I started to fly Delta to the same Latin America destinations.

The employee never made an empowered decision; she was probably not allowed to do so. Continental Airlines spends millions a month on advertising, just to get the attention of the few people who fly. Now, right in front of them is someone who flies constantly, and they destroy the relationship for about $100 in excess baggage fees. I avoided Continental for months.

Empowerment uses marketing money, and most companies seem to have an unlimited marketing budget. For some reason there's a disconnect between marketing money and **Empowerment**. Interestingly enough, when an employee makes an empowered decision it fuels word-of-mouth advertising, which is 10 times more effective and 10 times less expensive. In my mind, that's marketing money well spent. I have bought all my computers from Dell, but virtually no one can make an empowered decision at the company. You have to email Michael Dell to get an empowered decision based on common sense. With 96,000 employees, I have to email the CEO to get the problem solved?

This is the perfect example of a company that has lost it's focus on customer experience and lost billions of dollars in revenue. The stock value has dropped about 50 percent since Michael Dell originally retired in 2004. An empowered workforce at Dell could restore it's foundation of customer service and regain its number one ranking in PC sales worldwide.

Companies spend millions on the land, building the store, and stocking it full of product, all for one thing – the customer. But when the customer actually appears, they fall down on the job. All that time, thought, and money is wasted if the customer walks out, never to return. When a new Walgreens was scheduled to open near my home in Bloomington, Minnesota, I was thrilled. I had been waiting to switch my prescriptions from my current drugstore, which is slow, incompetent, and expensive, to a new place for quite sometime. Opening day, I was at Walgreens at 8:05 a.m., probably the second or third customer in the new store.

The assistant manger greeted me warmly as I came into the store. I inquired about the location of the pharmacy and the special offer for customers transferring their prescriptions. She said there weren't any special offers.

Usually, when a new retail drugstore opens up, it has incentives to get you to move your prescriptions to that store. The real money is made as people walk to the back of the store, buying other products before they pick up their prescription. I really wanted to switch, but I wanted a deal.

I asked if she could make an empowered decision. She said NO, she would be fired. (This was her first day on the job and most employees do not want to get fired, especially on day one.) She called the store manager, who appeared with another assistant manager. They said there is normally a $25 coupon, but they could not break store policy to give it to me. Then along came a District Manager, who could not make the big $25 decision either.

Four managers were unable to make a $25 empowered decision to make an immediate sale with long-term implications. Let's face it, if management will NOT make an empowered decision, there is little chance an employee will. The store manager said they were running an ad in the newspaper in two weeks. I should wait until then, clip the coupon, and bring it in to take advantage of the $25 special. I wanted to say, ***"You're kidding, right? There are over 20 pharmacies in the local area and you are letting someone who wants to become a loyal customer wait two weeks for a $25 discount."*** I didn't say anything; like most people, I just walked out.

No one appears to have been trained on customer service, customer experience, or **Empowerment**. The entire focus has been on advertising. Seldom do firms understand the power of a service strategy and how it fuels the most influential, least expensive form of advertising-- word of mouth. I started helping companies drive a service culture and train their employees on customer service back in 1980. Since then, I've noticed ALMOST all firms are addicted to advertising.

They never hesitate to spend a fortune on marketing and advertising. Walgreens in Bloomington will spend thousands of dollars on just one ad. I suspect the cost for each person who responds will be more than $50 a person, and that is before the $25 discount. If Walgreens went to the local newspaper, TV or radio station with $25 and wanted to buy a media campaign to attract new customers, how many words or seconds would it get on any of these media outlets?

Empowerment is marketing money. All employees should have one single objective each day, and that is to produce overhappy customers. It's really simple: smiling customers come back again and again and bring their friends, resulting in two very valuable assets to any company: customer loyalty and word-of-mouth advertising. Four managers in any organization who will not make a $25- empowered decision scares me. I would have been their first prescription customer and probably stayed with them for years, making regular purchases with long-term sales resulting in thousands of dollars in revenue.

I never did see the ad and didn't change to Walgreens. Instead, I transferred to my local supermarket's pharmacy. I am, however, still curious about how high you need to go in the Walgreens Corporation before you find someone who can make one tiny empowered decision.

So What is Empowerment?

2

Organizations say they want creative individuals, people who can think outside the box. They then insist that people submit resumes that are perfectly structured, touting the same qualifications of the people the company is getting rid of. They are moving these people out because of their inability to think outside the box. When will organizations realize that using the same standard hiring procedures is bound to get more of what they already have: blasé results. They need to adjust their procedures to attract the bold and brightest in their industry and support their success while they are there.

The goal of any company should be to hire people who aren't afraid to stand out. Unfortunately, the system is set up to hire those who fit in. It's like being in school and providing teachers with a series of mindless papers. Perfectly formatted, neatly organized, and filled with the same old dribble, they merely reiterate what they had just been told. The better one was at regurgitation, the higher one's grade.

Organizations and industries where equality is the norm depend heavily on **Empowerment**.

People who naturally gravitate to these companies and fields are empowered thinkers dedicated to bringing their best to the job every day. Often unable to be invisible, they are natural born problem solvers, consistently challenging the tried and true. Not satisfied to settle for mediocrity, they're the ones working overtime to come up with the perfect answer. They aren't even aware of the halfway mark at which most people stop.

The world economy is shifting. It threatens to leave behind the classic employee. No longer can the modern workforce expect security and comfort in positions that ask them only to come to work every day, keep their heads down, follow orders, and avoid risks. The next generation of workers must utilize all of their skills and talents to sell themselves to their customers and their employers every day and in every undertaking. The days of punching the clock and avoiding superiors are over. The future workforce will be more agile, creative, multitalented, and above all, empowered.

Empowerment helps you focus on making quick decisions on your own in order to ensure overhappy customers and to set yourself apart from the teeming masses angling for your job. An entire workforce of empowered employees will give your company a dramatic facelift and keep it competitive, strong, growing, and stable. You will be amazed at what **Empowerment** can do for you and your organization.

The definition of *"Empower"* is to give power or authority to, or to authorize. In the workplace, empowered employees have the power and the authority to make quick, informed, and on-the-fly decisions to help a customer, move a project forward, or solve a problem. When your company empowers you, it expects you to use all of your skills and all of the tools at your disposal to make a decision that benefits everyone involved… without having to consult with five different managers or supervisors. **Empowerment** puts you in control of your performance and tasks you with continuously improving and impressing on the job every day.

Consider your own worth. What is your true value to your company or any organization that might employ you in the future? How are you more than the suit or uniform you wear every day? How do you stand out in a crowd? How do you put your worth on display for all to see? Successful people and organizations utilize **Empowerment** to show off their talents and reach their goals. Those who reject **Empowerment** also fear risk. Employees who cling to the status quo will forever lag behind and be left in the dust.

Empowerment is all about creating an environment that gives employees the authority to make fast decisions to benefit customers. Empowered employees create happy customers and breed a culture of **empowerment** that infects every corner of a company.

Definition
em • pow • er (v):
to give power
or authority to;
to authorize

Empowerment means working quickly and efficiently.

Empowerment isn't just about power and authority; it's also about responsibility. Those with great power have just as great a responsibility to use their authority efficiently, appropriately, and to the greatest affect. Not only do you have the chance to decide, solve, and improve, you are now expected to do so on a daily basis, in every task or situation you encounter. You are responsible for utilizing your own talents and assimilating the significant information. You are challenged to make that one decision that will change someone's day, improve a timeworn process, or completely reinvent your company. Success in the economy of the future depends on thousands of those individually empowered decisions. That's the mark of innovation.

Use all of your education, humanity, common sense, and knowledge to jump into risky situations, quickly dissect problems, and make on-the-spot decisions. **Empowerment** gives you the authority to do whatever it takes.

"Power can be taken, but not given. The process of the taking is Empowerment in itself."
Gloria Steinem
American Activist and Writer

Empowerment also means working quickly and efficiently. The word *"slow"* does not fit into an empowered workplace or in your empowered decisions. Time is of the essence, and being able to make an empowered decision helps to rapidly move things along. Speed of thought, action, and consequence are the tools of the empowered worker. Without speed, the effects of your decisions will diminish. In a world where there is often so little time and so much to do, speed puts you front and center. Speed allows for maximum impact.

What is a life without **Empowerment** like? Imagine a world where no one makes decisions. Every employee passes the buck and moves a problem up the chain of command. It's a world where you dread coming to work, where you constantly fear being fired. It's a place where you slog through an endless calendar of eight-hour shifts, all for a paycheck, and where your talents go wasted; a universe where you blend into the crowd and are forgotten by history. A world without **Empowerment.** A life without **Empowerment** is a life unfulfilled.

Now consider the opposite. A world of **Empowerment** means loving what you do. It's coming to work every day and feeling wanted, needed, and valuable. You're encouraged to continually learn, interact, change, and remake yourself. It's using the best of your talents and skills to maximize your opportunities, make your mark, and fuel your future success. A life of **Empowerment** is a life fulfilled.

World Class Customer Service

Imagine a place where empowered employees consistently call you by name, leave hand-written notes upon arrival and departure, and even sing to you. Think about having each and every request greeted by a smile and positive attitude. Picture the "perfect 10" in customer service and you'll understand what I am talking about.

> *"You may never know what results come of your action, but if you do nothing, there will be no result."*
> Mahatma Gandhi
> *Pre eminent Political and Spiritual Leader of India*

With this level of service, you're probably envisioning a 5 star hotel on 5th Avenue in New York City, a luxury spa in Zurich, or in Dubai. Actually the ultimate in customer service can be found in Botswana, Namibia, Malawi, South Africa, Zambia, Zimbabwe, and Seychelles. Wilderness Safaris has it hands down over others in the hospitality, travel, and tourism industries; even those famous for service.

Headquartered in Johannesburg, South Africa and Maun, Botswana, Wilderness Safaris has 70 locations, with over 2700 employees (85 percent of which come from local rural communities around the conservation areas in which we work) in 7 countries. Formed 27 years ago, the company is committed to conservation, education, and customer experience. Keith Vincent, the Operations Director of Wilderness Safaris, manages the best and most consistent customer service I've ever seen. He understands that he is not in the travel or safari business, he is in the Customer Experience business. Very few people realize that they are in the customer experience business. At Wilderness Safaris they get it and I've never seen such depth of leadership throughout any organization.

In Botswana, with an unemployment rate of 30 percent, creating jobs is very important. The company's leases are dependent on increasing employment for the area's village people. The average salary is about $265 a month. Workers, more than 85 percent of which come from remote rural communities surrounding the areas they help to protect, remain at camp for three months at a time, followed by a one-month vacation.

All food and lodging is free. Often employees live better at work than they would in their own homes. The company pays employees airfare home for their month off. Wilderness Safaris has helped quiet, rather shy people become outgoing customer driven, empowered employees who love their job, the company, and the customers.

Most people enjoy a safari more for the wildlife. Participants concentrate on the following three areas to measure their customer experience while on safari.

> 1. *Guiding (Including the skill of the guides and the opportunity to view the animals.)*
>
> 2. *The facilities and the food (With 6 meals a day you can rapidly gain weight.)*
>
> 3. *Customer service.*

While the sleeping facilities were awesome, large, plush, better than any hotel suite, and the food delicious, the attitude of the employees was where the magic came alive.

We were always met at the small landing strips by our guides and then driven to the camps. Upon arrival we were greeted by management, who already knew our names, and the staff singing to us. We were given cold towels to clean our hands and face, then invited to enjoy a welcome drink. Employees introduced themselves and then asked our name. Throughout the stay, and at all locations the entire staff, including house keeping and kitchen help, used our name.

Everyone was smiling and friendly, and did everything in their power to make us feel special. We were offered a drink, and then told if the bartender was not there to just help ourselves. They would do whatever we wanted them to, for example, if our plane was leaving early, they would find us on the safari and take us to the airstrip. If we wanted to eat late or at different times, they would accommodate that also. Their policy is to do ANYTHING the customer wants. NO rules. NO policies, just an empowered staff focused on providing a great customer experience. Imagine my surprise when each pilot flew over Victoria Falls, 2-3 times, so I could take photos and a video. Whatever you want they work hard to accommodate you.

Have you ever been at a hotel or resort where each employee recognizes you, speaks to you by name, and is empowered to make your stay phenomenal?

Upon arrival and departure, hand-written notes with our names were left on our bed. When is the last time you received a personalized card upon your arrival and departure, let alone the staff singing to you?

If everyone reading this book could get their employees to master these skills they would dominate the market and dramatically increase sales.

I would rate the service at all the 6 camps I visited a "10." Wilderness Safaris offers the best consistent customer service I have experienced in my entire life. If you want a great customer experience or if you want to benchmark yourself against the best in the world, you should visit Wilderness Safaris. Look at their website at **www.wilderness-safaris.com**.

Many companies have great product and facilities, but rarely do they seem to care about employees. This was my 6th safari, the 3rd with Wilderness Safaris, and it is the ONLY safari operation that has truly mastered customer service. During the recent slowdown of the economy, Wilderness Safaris has remained dramatically stronger than its competition.

This is the perfect example of an empowered, customer service culture and how it supports a company's success.

Empowerment is A Way of Life that you will love.

Empowerment at its Best | 3

Very few CEOs in the world understand the service strategy. The most customer service-focused and successful CEO I know is Vernon W. Hill, II. In 1973, he founded Commerce Bank and sold it in 2007 to TD Bank Financial Group of Canada for $8.5 billion. Hill alone made over $400 million. Commerce Bank grew to 460 branches and $48 billion in assets. After selling Commerce Bank, the lack of **Empowerment** started to permeate and the service reputation Vernon Hill had worked hard to establish began to erode. He told me, *"It's now just a bank."*

Forbes magazine lists the American chief executives in the *"20-20-20 Club"* for 2007 — 20 years minimum in the job, 20 years minimum publicly traded shares, 20 percent minimum annual return. Hill is right behind Berkshire Hathaway's Warren Buffett and Oracle's Larry Ellison.

Recently, Hill started Metro Bank, London's first new bank in 153 years. As Metro Bank's co-founder and vice chairman, Hill predicts that Metro Bank will go from zero to $31 billion in deposits in 10 years with 200 stores. He is duplicating what Commerce Bank did in New York City. In September 2001, it opened with four stores in Manhattan. It interviewed 3,000 people to staff the first two locations. Of those, just 42 were hired. They were hired for attitudes and trained for skills. When Commerce Bank was sold, it had 250 stores in Greater New York and over $25 billion in deposits.

The average-sized bank branch in America has $50 million in deposits; Commerce Bank had $120 million. The median new-bank branch grows to $19 million in deposits in five years; Commerce Bank averaged $87 million.

Commerce Bank was the most customer-driven bank in the United States. The secret of Commerce Bank was its ability to get the highest deposit growth at the lowest cost. This requires creating and maintaining an emotional attachment with the customer. Hill plans to duplicate this scenario at Metro Bank. Hill builds banks by treating every customer royally. His focus is on creating fans, not just customers. Great customer service comes through a business model focused on building *"Fans not Customers."* Metro Bank, London, will bring this philosophy to a market devoid of customer service.

Vernon Hill built a company around **Empowerment**. The number one rule at Hill's banks is that every employee is empowered to say *"yes"* to customers, but two are required to say *"no."* Employees don't hide behind bank policy to avoid helping customers. If an employee has to say no, wants to say no, or even believes no is the right decision, he has to go to someone with greater authority, who can waive a rule, make sense out of what the customer wants, or come up with a more palatable solution. This philosophy empowers team members to say *"Yes!"* to customers.

Hill said, *"At traditional banks, it takes an act of God to get a fee waived. Employees must get senior management review and approval, or they will die."* At Commerce Bank, and now at Metro Bank, team members have the freedom to do the right thing for customers and for shareholders.

Hill built a bank with over 15,000 employees. At Commerce Bank they understood service recovery. He said, *"Recovery is an art."* Hill sees errors as an opportunity to strengthen a customer relationship with immediate resolution through empowered team members and a *"Satisfaction Guarantee"* plan.

He had built a power retailer. He sees himself as a retailer, not a banker. The same success he had in the United States will work in Britain. Metro Bank will be the most successful bank in London. It will achieve incredible financial results, because everywhere in the world customers love getting great service from empowered employees.

Hill said, *"Without customers, nobody has a job."* No CEO in the world better understands this message and walks the talk. Most CEOs send out a memo and wash their hands of customer service.

Customer service is the only strategy you can implement anywhere in the world and your competition will not copy you. No one copied Commerce Bank in the United States and NO one will copy Metro Bank in London. Hill has a better grasp of the power of customer service and **Empowerment** than any CEO in the world and will once again prove that money falls from the skies when you implement the service strategy. More importantly, with the service strategy and **Empowerment**, you have at least a 10 year lead time over your competition.

I'm not sure why CEOs don't follow Hill's lead. Maybe it's just too much work, or the strategies are a bit too soft for them to deal with.

The purpose of this book is to empower employees. If you're in management, you need to push **Empowerment** everyday, by continuously and consistently looking for ways to celebrate and recognize empowered employees. Everytime you see an employee bending the rules, make a big deal out of it. You should make it known throughout the organization and put it in your company newsletter. People are driven more by recognition than by money. The goal is to get employees to make instinctive, empowered decisions. It will take years to get them to that point. It's the single most difficult thing to accomplish in customer service, so much so that I created a training program titled **Empowerment: A Way of Life** specifically to teach the art of **Empowerment** to the total workforce. It can be viewed at our website **www.customer-service.com**

The book you're reading should ideally be given
to every single employee in the organization
in an effort to address and overcome the four
challenges that all businesses face. They are:

First   *Many executives don't*
                    trust the customer.
                    They feel that customers
                    are lying and cheating.
                    They believe the
                    customer is trying to
                    take advantage of them.
                    Employees feel the same way.

Second   *We don't trust employees.*
                    We pay them as little as we
                    can and have even less
                    confidence in their ability to
                    make decisions. We have a
                    belief that our lying, cheating
                    customers are going to take
                    advantage of our
                    incompetent employees.

Third   *With Empowerment*
                    you don't need as many
                    managers and supervisors.
                    They're not overly excited about
                    losing their perceived power,
                    nor are they thrilled about
                    the potential of losing their jobs.

Fourth   *Very few employees are*
                    on their knees at night
                    praying for Empowerment.
                    It's just too risky.

All of these challenges need to be overcome to reach **Empowerment**. The single objective of any company should be to have overhappy customers. If you do that, you'll make a fortune. So many things happen during the day that are so unpredictable, they require employees to make empowered decisions and to bend rules, policies and procedures to be successful.

Imagine the efficiency of governments encouraging empowerment of their workforces. The following is an example of just that:

Taking Some of the Sting Out of Paying Taxes

In an empowered world, friendly people would accept your tax money, then use it wisely.

The Tanzania Revenue Authority was the winner of Service Quality Institute's International 2009 Client of the Year Award, and I asked its Commissioner General, Harry Kitillya, to give us some insight on how the TRA uses empowerment to improve customer service and increase revenue.

Internal revenue agencies seem to be the antithesis of customer service in my mind. In the United States we call that agency the IRS, and its employees are the last people we want to hang out with or smooze with at a party. Yet here is an example of how they use a service strategy to increase revenue. It is very rare to find a CEO of any government organization that understands the power of customer service and the service strategy.

In 2003, Commissioner General Kitillya had his top two people attend my first open seminar in Kenya. Over the course of the next several years, he had me deliver two service strategy seminars for his leadership teams. In addition to private presentations, he has sent many on his management team to my public service strategy seminars in Tanzania. He has been using Service Quality Institute programs to change the culture of his 3,000-employee workforce.

In a very short time he and his staff have been able to make dramatic changes to their organization. He is passionate about customer service and empowerment and how they work hand in hand to create overhappy customers. I believe he is one of the most customer focused government officials in Africa. This is what he has to say about this ongoing project:

Modern business organizations can best survive with focused strategies and goals. These strategies must be implemented by a workforce of capable employees making timely decisions. The main goal of workers should support and enhance the performance of the organization.

Tanzania Revenue Authority (TRA), whose main function is to assess and collect taxes, was established in 1996. The old tax administration operated under strict government rules and regulations. The system was inflexible, civil servants had no authority, and making even small changes was a lengthy and costly process. Bureaucracy ruled and everyone suffered.

Soon after being established, the TRA and its new tax administration was empowered to make its own operational rules and regulations. We were now able to build systems centered on the needs and expectations of the customers/ taxpayers as well as the employees. This degree of autonomy was the first step of improvement in tax administration.

While making the initial infrastructural improvements, particularly the office buildings where taxpayers pay their taxes, the Authority looked to its human capital. Knowing it needed a staff that could perform well, its goal was to have a skilled and agile workforce that could make empowered decisions. Yearly customer service focused training programs were implemented. Employees were trained on technical areas, management, and service delivery. The overall strategy was to assist workers in modernizing administration and make it more responsive to taxpayers.

New rules and regulations, along with innovative tax laws such as Value Added Tax (VAT), were introduced. Logistical changes offered taxpayers better service. Decentralization allowed payments to be made at banks. A specific department was established for taxpayers of significant amounts to ensure speed, accuracy, and ease of facilitating large transactions. These adjustments removed unnecessary bureaucracy, improved customer relations, and created a greater need for confident, trustworthy employees. These workers were empowered to discuss with taxpayers their audit findings and even waive penalties for mistakes.

Since its establishment, Tanzania Revenue Authority has been receiving feedback with a view to improving the quality of services that it provides to its customers.

Service Quality Institute of Minneapolis, Minnesota, in the USA, was engaged to train staff on the etiquettes of quality customer service, specifically on Speed in Service Delivery, Customer Loyalty, and Service Recovery. The training managed to change the negative mindset of the staff on the importance of customer service to taxpayers.

Another big milestone in service delivery was the adaptation of Quality Management System (QMS), ISO 9001:2000. Having the ISO 9001:2008 Certification as an institution provides automated quality services to its customers based on international standards.

The TRA is now more customer centric, with processes and measures that meet and often exceed international standards. The impact of the improved services can be reflected in the steadily increasing revenue collection. Each year the average has risen in monthly collection from Tshs 75 billion ($48.6 million USD) in 1998/99 to Tshs 370 billion ($243 million USD) in 2009/10.

Under our policy of continuous improvement of services to our customers, TRA employees can now reach their potential by embracing their responsibilities and authority without fear of making mistakes. They are encouraged to bend rules and regulations to make customer focused decisions for the better performance of the organization.

TRA shall not be complacent with the achievements gained with regard to customer service delivery. We shall implement a Service Culture Program under the third Corporate Plan where all employees will be trained on new skills and approaches on service delivery.

We embrace empowerment as way of life in the Tanzania Revenue Authority. We believe that having an empowered workforce with employees prepared to bend the rules in favor of customers is so much better than having stagnant and conservative individuals who put brakes on progress.

Harry M Kitillya
Commissioner General

Congratulations to Commissioner General Kitillya and all the empowered employees at the Tanzania Revenue Authority. You have figured out how to take some of the sting out of paying taxes. Wouldn't it be awesome if all government leaders mastered service strategy and encouraged empowerment? We'd see a more efficient use of tax dollars and, if governments were more customer driven, millions of taxpayers around the world would be overhappy.

In 1979, I decided to write a program on customer service, because I saw companies spending a fortune on marketing, trying to drive customers to their place of business. As the customers arrived, I saw them hit the customers on the head with a baseball bat to make sure they didn't come back. In January 1980, I released Feelings, the world's first customer service program. Since then I've spent millions of dollars adding new programs and updating programs that change attitudes and behaviors.

Without repetition and reinforcement there's little chance to create a service culture. Service Quality Institute has enough products to introduce something new and fresh every four to six months for over three consecutive years.

Too many firms buy one program or one book and believe they're finished. There's no magic training program or book. You don't graduate from college by taking one class; it's a process and a structured curriculum. The most important asset in any organization is its employees, and consistently across the world they are the least paid, least trained and least appreciated.

Supervisors and managers need to be trained on how to push and reinforce **Empowerment**. If a supervisor ever fires an employee for making an empowered decision, word will spread within 24 hours and it'll take years to recover. Realize that perception is reality and employees don't want to lose their job. The purpose of the book is to help CEOs, executives, and enlightened employees to develop a truly empowered workforce, and to crush the competition. Many employees don't believe in themselves. This book is designed to get people to think differently about themselves, their company and their customers.

Service leaders have employees who are productive, think on their own, and are empowered versus just showing up and working. Mediocre employees are very expensive. High-performing employees make you lots of money.

"In reality, I believe that any company is only as good as its least empowered employee!

Why Should I Care About Empowerment?

4

Over time, most workers have been trained to ignore **Empowerment**, even to run away from the responsibility. For all of the success and innovation that industrialization introduced into modern manufacturing, it did little to cultivate creative thinkers and decision makers. Employees on the assembly line were paid a decent wage to not ask questions and to not think outside of the one function they were tasked to perform, over and over and over again. Repetition reigned supreme. The result was an efficient workflow that favored production and the manufactured product over all else.

In today's economy, you and your talents are the commodity most in demand from consumers. Ideas and creativity are the fuel of the future. The worker who has spent a lifetime avoiding risk and not cultivating his imagination has to work even harder to catch up. **Empowerment** is a game-changing tool that cannot hurt you; it will only help you.

It's a busy world. People are always in a hurry. **Empowerment** allows you to process information and make decisions quickly – in line with today's fast-paced lifestyles.

Empowerment makes your job easier!

Being empowered increases your chance of success by putting your skills and talents on display for all to see, especially your managers and supervisors. **Empowerment** simplifies your job by placing you in charge of your own performance and giving you the responsibility to improve your work. It dramatically enhances customer experiences for you and your customers. **Empowerment** allows you to be assertive and get things done faster than before. It puts you in control of your life and allows you to improve others' lives as well. Choose **Empowerment** to make your job easier and more rewarding day in and day out.

Empowerment allows you to show your employers what you are truly capable of accomplishing. It is a platform to demonstrate your competence and decision-making abilities under pressure. Employees who make empowered decisions stand out from the group and are noticed by their superiors. Empowered employees force employers to take notice of their excellent work and the contribution they make to the environment of productivity and efficiency that is fundamental to a thriving organization.

Employers will see you as empowered and notice your talent. They will want to promote you, or at the very least they will hold you up as an example to everyone else at your organization.

Just imagine what your company could do with an entire workforce of empowered employees ready to do whatever it takes to succeed. Your superiors will fall all over themselves trying to keep you happy and outperforming the competition.

For example, at the Ritz Carlton hotel chain, each quarter five employees are recognized by the company for their *"5-star behavior."* This signifies service where staff has gone out of their way to help customers. These lucky employees are rewarded with $500 each. Additionally, one of the 20 quarterly winners is awarded a free round trip ticket to any Ritz Carlton in the world, as well as $8,500 in cash. Not a bad reward for a little empowered decision-making, is it?

Think about your job. Do you feel stuck? How many of your colleagues have been hired and promoted around you? Do you feel like your supervisors are noticing you? Take a moment to think about what sets you apart? What skills do you have that could make a difference? Empower yourself to find out. Think about your job and how you could highlight your value to the company. Analyze how your colleagues made names for themselves and moved up. Most importantly, consider what it takes to stand out at your organization. **Empowerment** creates opportunities for you to significantly emphasize your worth and bring your talents to the forefront of your performance. Creativity, assertiveness, speed, constant self-improvement, and **Empowerment** all play a part in your continued success.

Empowerment will help you advance your career. Empowered employees are more likely to get raises and promotions. Employees who reject **Empowerment** remain stagnant.

Empowerment will help advance your career.

Empowerment has strong benefits for the company. Organizations that rely on the skills and talents of their empowered employees save money and time, increase profits, and maintain strong customer satisfaction. **Empowerment** keeps customers happy and loyal. In turn, their happiness spreads to new customers. Let's not forget who benefits when a company's fortunes improve: you, the employee - as the potential for promotions, salary increases, expanded responsibilities, and worker satisfaction are all greatly enhanced.

Information Is the Key! 5

Start by gathering information. Only then can you be empowered. Get to know your company, your customers, and yourself. Learn everything possible about your job. Don't stop at the products or services you sell. Understand the big picture, as well as your role in the entire business cycle. If you're selling a product, learn how it's made. Find out how it's inventoried and how it compares to other products of its kind. To be empowered you need to take responsibility for seeking out information – you can't wait for it to come to you. Remember, knowledge is power.

Show your company that you share and support its vision. Make it known that you want to absorb all there is to know about the business. Your organization will appreciate your initiative and support your desire to be informed. The more you know about the company, your customers and your position, the better equipped you will be when called upon to create and innovate. You'll be able to successfully repurpose the information to meet your own needs, the requirements of your customers, and the goals of your organization.

The more you know about your company, the better equipped you are to problem solve and to innovate.

Let's say you hear that your organization is going to update a line of products that you regularly use and really like. There is nothing wrong with showing your company how excited you are about the new products. You demonstrate your responsibility and desire by sharing what you know. This will send an important message to your company. It will show how interested you are in the organization and the products that you provide. It will also create an opportunity for you to learn more about the products, which will in turn help you when others ask questions about them.

Strive to learn as much as you can about your company.

Keep your eyes and ears open for new policies or procedures at your organization. Being empowered means seeking out change. Embrace it. You will continue to learn all you can about your company and how the business is run, while dramatically increasing your value. This knowledge will provide additional opportunities for you to suggest well-thought-out modifications to policies or procedures.

Think about how you shop. The more information you have, the better equipped you are to make a good decision. If you want to buy a car, where would you start? You might do some research on the Internet about different types of cars that strike your interest and are within your price range. You would probably read some automobile reports or ask your friends, family members, or co-workers if they have any experience with specific models. Then you might look a little more closely at the price, search for deals, discounts, or tax credits.

After you have done the research, you would go to the dealership and test drive several of the cars at the top of your list. The homework you've done would make you more likely to find the car that's right for you once you hit the showroom floor. You certainly wouldn't go in there and wing it without having any knowledge or information about the car. You would probably end up with a vehicle out of your price range that doesn't meet your needs.

The same strategy goes for your job. You need to be equipped with knowledge. A big part of being prepared is being informed. Empower yourself to seek out information.

- *What are your responsibilities?*

- *What do you produce?*

- *How are you expected to perform?*

- *What areas can you expand upon?*

- *Where could you make improvements?*

Empowered employees are never satisfied with the status quo. They are always looking for ways to improve and exceed expectations.

It's not enough to ask questions; seek out information using every possible resource. You should have a voracious appetite. Information is your lifeblood. It's the key to your success and satisfaction in the workplace. Strive to learn as much as possible about your company, the industry, and the competition. Studying the industry provides ample time to solve your company's future regulation challenges. Knowing how your company does things is great, but imagine your value when you understand how the competition works. Before long you'll be several steps ahead of your customers and other employees, ensuring your success in the process.

It's All About Trust! 6

For you to succeed and thrive as an empowered employee, you have to trust that your organization, your co-workers, and your customers will be there to back you. Trust must exist on three levels.

The Mayo Clinic in Rochester, Minnesota, is the Ritz Carlton of the health care industry. Service is the cornerstone of Mayo's culture. A foundation of sophisticated systems supports employee **empowerment,** while training ensures superior customer service delivery. Accuracy, efficiency, and speed are just some of the features that have made Mayo Clinic world famous.

Often, it's the simple things that make a difference to customers. When I wanted to move my eye doctor appointment to a day earlier, I just stopped by and they quickly adjusted my schedule to get me in. A centralized internal system allows employees the flexibility to react immediately to customer's requests. In many cases, there is no additional expense to providing exceptional customer service.

Trust is imperative in order to make Empowerment successful.

Another time, when leaving the Mayo parking garage, I could not find my parking ticket. In most lots, if you lose your ticket you are forced to pay for the entire day. At Mayo, the employee said, *"Don't worry about it"*. I paid for the two hours I was there. What is the big deal? Will a billion-dollar health care facility go broke because it believed the customer? NO! By the way, this is the same parking garage that 15 months later helped an older couple get their dead car battery jumped for free.

The Mayo Clinic has created an environment of **Empowerment** based on trust. Employees are empowered to use their best judgment and all available resources to produce overhappy customers. Mayo Clinic has become world-renowned for providing both top-notch health care AND impeccable customer service.

You need to trust your employers and they need to trust you.

First, your employers must trust you. They hired you. They chose you from a list of applicants for a reason. Why else would they pay you to do a job and trust you to do it well? From the company's perspective, it made a decision that you were the right person to do the work. Therefore, it must trust you to do the job.

When a company empowers its employees, it trusts them to make decisions on its behalf. For example, let's say you work for a construction company. You've been awarded a huge contract. Your crew runs out of a roofing substrate, which brings the entire operation to a halt. The company trusts your abilities to make the decisions necessary to keep the job moving and the clients happy. If you feel the need to call your manager or some other supervisor, then the process has already been hampered. If your organization puts its trust in you, you must trust it as well.

The second area of trust is on your end. Trust is a two-way street. You need to trust your employer, your company, but most of all yourself. When you're well prepared, responsible, and empowered, you must have confidence in your ability to choose the best possible outcome.

If you are tasked with making empowered decisions, you must trust that you have the authority and responsibility to do so. When presented with a project or a problem, act quickly and decisively. Break it down to its relevant parts, and gather all of the pertinent information you need without being told. Usually a clear, solution will become obvious after you have done some research, but if it doesn't, make a decision based on your expertise. Trust that your company has faith in you; it values your skills and put you in position of authority for a reason. If you sit around wondering and debating, afraid to take a step in any direction, you work against that trust and bring the entire enterprise to a halt.

Let's say your manager tells you to purchase some photo quality paper for a print job. He gives you the company credit card and says he trusts you to make the right choice. Your company trusts you.

"The glue that holds all relationships together – including the relationship between the leader and the led is trust, and trust is based on integrity."
Brian Tracy
American Speaker, Trainer, and Self-help Author

*"The chief
lesson I
learned in a
long life is that
the only way
to make a
man
trustworthy
is to trust
him; and the
surest way
to make him
untrustworthy
is distrust him
and show him
your distrust."*
Henry L.
Stimson
*American,
Statesman*

At the office supply store you see hundreds of options and brands. As you stand confused by the sheer variety and all the different specific uses, you debate which you should buy. You might consider calling your manager to get further instructions, but he just put his faith in you. He values your experience and expertise to make a logical, rational decision. Your indecisiveness slows things down. You need to feel empowered to make the decision he trusted you to make. Seize the moment; trust your company and the authority it has given you to make an empowered decision.

The third type of trust that must exist is between you and yourself. Some call it confidence. Your company trusts you. You trust your company. Now it's time to trust yourself. Indecisiveness, insecurity, and a lack of clarity – these feelings can hamper a project or a decision. But even more, a lack of confidence in your own abilities can send a task bounding off the tracks. No one is more aware of your capabilities than you are. You know what you bring to the table. You know what you're good at and where you need to improve. You need to be honest with yourself and use your knowledge, skills and talents to find creative ways to solve problems or accomplish tasks. Trust that your employer has made the right decision by placing his trust in you. Your company, your management, will evaluate you – give you feedback to facilitate continuous improvement.

Trust that your decision carries with it the authority your organization has bestowed upon you. While a necessary tool to get the job done, authority is a symbol of the direct trust an organization places in its most valued employees. Use it wisely to get the job done and adjust your goals accordingly.

The existence and reinforcement of trust between you and your company will strengthen the empowered decisions you make. The faith you have in yourself will surely improve the outcomes from those decisions while dramatically increasing your chances of success.

The happier a customer is, the better and easier your job is to do.

Give Me Some Feedback!   7

You may be your own biggest fan and your harshest critic, but the opinions of others count – especially when they help evaluate your performance in the workplace. You get better at making empowered decisions by soliciting feedback from your supervisors, co-workers, and customers. Like gathering information, being empowered means being proactive, assertive, and responsible. Don't wait to get feedback – seek it out. Feedback is a vital cog in the machine of an empowered workforce.

Consider the following scenario. You complete a massive project that required weeks of planning followed by a month of execution. Finally, you finish the project, breathe a sigh of relief, submit it for review, and wait. You wait for what seems like an eternity, but you hear nothing. Eventually, you give up waiting, somewhat daunted by the fact that you never heard a single word after all that work. Soon, you move on to a new and similarly demanding project. You tackle it with the same gusto and creativity. Right or wrong, your decisions are shaped by the ones you've made on previous projects. After working even harder and longer, you submit it. The next day your boss calls you in and details all of the mistakes with the project.

He is quick to point out how they mirror the same inconsistencies you made on the last project. Not at all what you were expecting, this kind of exchange leaves you feeling angry and frustrated.

Feedback is a vital cog in the Empowerment machine.

What just happened, you ask yourself? What's going on here? You never received any feedback on the first project and now find yourself completely confused. How were you supposed to know you were making the same mistakes on the second project? Without timely feedback, there would have been no reason to alter your strategy and reevaluate the empowered decisions you made the first time around.

The only way to know if you're working within expectations is to seek out feedback. Ideally, your manager will take the time to let you know how you're doing, but we don't live in an ideal world. If you're not getting the feedback you need to educate yourself and improve your outcomes, step forward and ask! By taking responsibility, you'll perform at a higher level, get better overall results, and be happier. No longer operating in a vacuum, you'll have improved chances of success. The best part is that you'll feel empowered.

Let's say a few weeks have passed since your manager told you she wanted you to use your skills to make more empowered decisions in the workplace. You might feel that you have been doing so, but have yet to hear anything positive or negative about your performance. You wonder if you are going too far, or maybe you aren't going far enough. There's nothing wrong with asking your manager how she feels about your performance and what you need to work on.

Seeking out feedback demonstrates your desire to continuously improve. You will show your company, supervisors, and customers that you are not complacent nor are you willing to settle for mediocrity. This one simple act can make all the difference: instead of waiting for feedback, seek it out.

Get proactive with your approach on the job. If you encounter a problem during one project that could recur in others, say something. Work to change the procedure or process so that the product is better next time. Don't just stand back and wait for things to happen. Grab the bull by the horns. Get out ahead of projects. Devise strategies for improving your speed and accuracy. Develop productive relationships with co-workers who can help you. Head off potential problems well before they derail a project. Anticipate your customers' needs, and empower yourself to find solutions.

Just as important as soliciting feedback is how you react when you receive it. Make sure that you listen and pay close attention to what a manager or supervisor tells you. When someone takes the time to provide you with valuable information, the least you can do is listen. But **Empowerment** isn't about the *"least"* you can do. The most you can do is absorb the criticism. Dissect your performance and the feedback you receive. What did you do right, and how did you come to those conclusions? What did you do wrong, and how can you improve?

If you're not getting feedback, ask!

Feedback is a vital ingredient in becoming the best, most productive, and valuable worker you can be. Seek it out often and utilize it wisely.

"Criticism is something we can avoid easily by saying nothing, doing nothing and being nothing."
Aristotle
Ancient Greek Philosopher, Scientist, and Physician

Receiving feedback, particularly when it is negative, can be difficult for anyone. Don't get defensive – you've been empowered to do a job. You won't get fired for making an empowered decision. Your employer is giving you feedback to help you learn and grow as well as to increase the company's success. Consider positive and negative criticism equally. Take it upon yourself to improve in the areas that were targeted for development. Design a plan of action and timeline for making the necessary improvements. Share these goals with your employer and thank them for their investment in your growth. Celebrate positive feedback. Take a few moments to congratulate yourself on your achievement. Bask in the glory of **Empowerment** and its role in your success.

Remember, **Empowerment** depends on you taking the initiative. That means constantly striving to be a better employee. There is no limit to what you can do when you remove the self-imposed limitations: moving up, making more money. Feedback, whether you acquire it or it's given freely, will help you get there.

Don't get defensive.

A Little Help, Please! 8

You are empowered. Your company has given authority to you and expects you to make the necessary decisions to generate success. Part of the power that you now have is the ability to delegate authority to others and ask for help when you feel you need it.

The ability to ask for help and delegate authority is not a sign of weakness. It does not tell others that you cannot perform or that you are falling behind. Delegation and engagement are the cornerstones of teamwork, an approach that ensures things will continue to run smoothly and efficiently even at the busiest and most difficult times. Empower yourself to ask for help or to get others involved. An empowered team is exponentially more effective than an empowered individual.

Let's say you work at a bank. You notice the customer line has become unreasonably long. Tempers are beginning to flair. It's a matter of moments before the grumbling is directed to you and your co-workers. So what do you do?

"How far would Moses have gone if he had taken a poll in Egypt?"
Harry S. Truman
33rd President of the United States

- *Ignore the long line and focus on your job.*

- *Imagine that those customers aren't there and let their laser beam stares pass right through you. This accomplishes nothing other than guaranteeing a line of unhappy customers, an afternoon of grumpy co-workers, and a weekend trying to make up for an inefficient couple of hours.*

You might be empowered to make the decision to do nothing, but you have a responsibility to do whatever it takes to remedy the situation for everyone. Attack the problem and ask for help if you need it. Request that another window be opened. Call a co-worker back from break a little early. Move someone from the drive-through to the counter for a couple of minutes. Get creative and don't let roadblocks prevent customer satisfaction.

By delegating authority or asking for help in situations like the one above, you emphasize your own ability to handle chaos and deliver order in a hectic situation. You have just made an empowered decision that will benefit everyone.

Delegate authority, but don't be bossy.

Now, there is a fine line between delegating authority and being bossy, as well as asking for help and being needy. You should strive to treat your co-workers as equals while respecting your own abilities.

When you need co-worker assistance, get their buy-in on the project or problem. You seek help from others because you respect their individual areas of expertise. Make them know that their involvement is essential to a successful outcome. Speak to your fellow employees or supervisors in ways that will make them want to help. This attitude underscores the trust you have in their judgment, the value you place in their skills, and ensures your willingness to help them in the future.

Finally, give credit where credit is due. If someone helps you complete a project or solve a thorny issue, make it known to others that she was a valuable resource. This increases her standing with her co-workers and with the company and improves your image in the eyes of your colleagues as a team player.

Empower yourself to delegate authority. Ask for help when you need it. You can keep your organization running smoothly, your customers happy, and your co-workers willing and able to put their skills on the line for you.

"There is only one boss: The customer. And he can fire anybody in the company from the chairman on down, simply by spending his money somewhere else."
Sam Walton
American, Founder of Wal-Mart

I'm Afraid! 9

So why isn't every employee empowered? Why don't we all utilize our creativity, knowledge, and expertise to reinvent ourselves and innovate on the job? It seems like a no-brainer.

The reality is quite the opposite. There are several perceived barriers that have made **Empowerment** difficult to achieve in the past. However, when you meet each barrier head on, you'll see that they can easily be overcome.

Hey, I Need This Job!

Fear is both an extremely powerful and a debilitating emotion. It can inhibit your ability to make empowered and responsible decisions on the job or in your life. Fear can hold you back and keep you from reaching your true potential. When you live in a state of apprehension, you cannot get better at what you do, make personal improvements, or reach your goals. Sure, you may be comfortable with the way things are.

> *"Fear defeats more people than any one thing in the world."*
> Ralph Waldo Emerson
> *American Poet and Philosopher*

You could be reluctant to rock the boat, telling yourself that you're safe being invisible. This type of attitude, while common, is deadly. It wastes time, squanders opportunities, and destroys chances for advancement. Without **Empowerment** you'll be stuck, unless you have the confidence to jump in, take a risk, and be recognized. Taking chances and putting your doubts to the test keeps you ahead of the curve; fear only leaves you bringing up the rear.

Fear is the reason most employees have rejected Empowerment in the past.

Most employees reject **Empowerment** out of fear. They have been told for the balance of their working lives that they should toe the line, avert their eyes, and keep their ideas to themselves. They rely on that 9 to 5 schedule and the monotonous routine that keeps them safely cocooned in a banal and unfulfilled working existence. They need their jobs and they feel that the best way to keep them is to stay out of the way and let the steamroller of business pass them by. These employees feel that empowered decisions lead to one thing: the unemployment line. They left a passion for their job and their imaginations behind long ago and are more than willing to suffer through decades of complacency for the steady delivery of a modest salary. It is safer for them to just go on doing their job without taking any risks or chances.

I can understand being cautious, but this example is just plain crazy.

After I had paid a Washington Mutual credit card in full, I got a statement with a balance of $1.56. I called the customer service line and was told by the representative that it was an interest charge. I said if the charge was not removed I would cut up the card and mail it back. She said she had to talk to her supervisor to get approval.

I asked, *"You don't have permission to waive $1.56 fee?"* She said she did, but needed to talk to her supervisor.

When an employee cannot make an empowered $1.56 decision, it is really bad. She was able to get her supervisor's approval. Amazing.

With this level of employee **Empowerment**, no wonder Washington Mutual is now owned by JP Morgan Chase.
We need to look closely at the decisions that employees are afraid to make. Consider for a moment the extent that some people are underperforming at their jobs. Are they checked out and going through the motions everywhere or just at work? It's important to understand that systems are set up to facilitate their absence of engagement and perpetuate their lack of **Empowerment**.

   • *What kind of life is that?*

   • *Where's the fire for success?*

   • *Where's the appetite for a challenge?*

Not only do modern workers crave diversity and challenge in the workplace, but companies also need and expect them to be innovative on the job. It's a deadening cycle. Employees play it safe and are passed over by the unrelenting march of economic evolution. Companies refuse to change and reinvent, and they are also being left in history's wake in record numbers.

Here's a terrific example of a company that fired an employee for making an empowered decision – and how that company suffered the consequences:

Firing an employee for making an empowered choice in favor of a customer is one of the worst decisions that any CEO, business owner or supervisor can make. Let's take the example of an Atlantic Subway Ltd franchise in Dartmouth, Nova Scotia, Canada. The story goes like this: Heidi Heise was let go for giving away a foot-long sandwich to neighbors left homeless and hungry after an apartment fire.

When the two men showed up at her workplace to thank her, Heise gave them a couple of subs. *"I knew they had no food, no money and nowhere to live, so I gave them each a six-inch sub,"* Heise explained. But, when she went to work the next day, she was fired for giving away the subs. *"They were like, We went over the cameras and we (saw) you on the weekend, give away a free sub, she said".* The two six-inch subs are the equivalent of one 12-inch sub, which Subway employees are entitled to as a staff lunch, which must be marked down.

Clearly, not every owner or boss understands the power of customer service and **Empowerment**. The sandwich was valued at about $6 with a cost of goods of approximately $1. Hundreds of thousands of people in Canada and across the world heard about the firing.

The $1 sub probably generated upwards of $100,000 in negative publicity for Subway.

How much does Subway spend on marketing? It costs a small fortune just to get a customer in the door. When you finally have one there, shouldn't you do whatever you can to keep them coming back? In a time of great need and an opportunity to show compassion, Heise was there to support these victims in a way that could have resulted in loyal, lifelong customers. Considering a marketing budget, this is a minuscule investment. Imagine if Subway went to the local media in Dartmouth, Nova Scotia with $1 and said, *"We want to run a media campaign, to attract more customers."* How much air time or print space would they get?

Congratulations to Quiznos franchisee Steve Webber. *"Heidi is a person who was trying to do the right thing,"* Webber said. *"I heard about the story and, as luck would have it, my store had an opening... I thought it was great timing, so we tracked her down to see if she was interested. These are the kind of people Quiznos likes to have working in our stores."*

Quiznos got a great employee and virtually priceless publicity. Subway lost an incredible asset, and Heidi found a better place to work, where **Empowerment** and great service are valued.

Overhappy customers should be the objective of every firm, and empowered employees like Heidi are worth their weight in gold.

> *"Too many of us are not living our dreams because we are living our fears."*
> Les Brown
> *American Motivational Speaker, and Author*

Don't Yell at Me

OK, so maybe you do not fear being fired. However, some still reject **Empowerment** because they are afraid of the responsibility that comes with it. Employees who fear making the wrong decision or have no confidence in their own ability drain **Empowerment** of its force and effectiveness. Now, more than ever, your company wants and needs you to make empowered decisions.

Making incorrect decisions is all part of the learning process. Use those instances to improve your strategy for success moving forward. Do not bury your head in the sand and avoid taking risks in the future. Ninety percent of the time, empowered employees make decisions in the best interest of their companies and themselves. The nuances of right and wrong can be tweaked for future reference.

"Listen to what you know instead of what you fear."
Richard David Bach
American, Author of Jonathan Livingston Seagull

If your heart, head, and intentions are in the right place, your company will stand behind you, because its creative capital is you. Despite the popular misconception, your supervisors are eager for you to make empowered decisions. Their success is dependent on you taking responsibility for yourself and putting the company's goals first every time you act. Of course, there might be some bumps in the road, but a majority of the time the information you have at your disposal will be more than enough to create virtually limitless positive outcomes.

If a mistake is made, the best thing your manager can do is to tell you where you went astray in a constructive manner. This is a terrific opportunity to work together to evaluate the situation and create an action plan for the future. This comes back to trust. You must have faith in your company's trust in you. Managers know that no one is perfect and mistakes are made from time to time. You must have confidence that, whatever happens, no one will bite your head off. Anger, as well as fear of failure, are counterproductive and accomplish nothing. Failing on every level, anger actually hinders improvement and development.

If you do find yourself on the receiving end of a tongue lashing, remain calm. It's extremely important not to get confrontational. Start by listening with an open mind. Calmly ask for specific details of what mistakes were made. This is not a time to accept generalities; seek explicit points of reference and clear examples. Make sure you understand precisely what the manager or supervisor is referring to and the exact issue with your actions.

When it's your turn, clearly state what guided your decisions. Offer specific facts, analysis, and timelines that led to your conclusion. Make it known that, regardless of the outcome, your decision was based on sound judgment. Ultimately, it was motivated by your desire for success. Your overriding goal, with this and every decision, is to improve the outcome for the company and the customer. Most managers will be impressed with your skills at handling difficult situations, respect

You and your company are seeking success on every level.

your ability to analyze and decide quickly, and come away with a better understanding of the value you bring to the company. A smart manager will tap your dedication and harness it for future success. Managers and supervisors who can't, or won't, adapt to an empowered workforce will experience an erosion of power and will eventually be removed from any position of authority.

"The greatest mistake you can make in life is to be continually fearing that you will make one."

Elbert Hubbard
American Writer, Publisher, Artist, and Philosopher

Fear leads to counterproductive situations that paralyze workers. Customers get upset. Orders back up. Managers get nervous. Stock prices tumble. Employees are unhappy because they have to deal with increasingly difficult situations that they feel powerless to affect. And the employer is unhappy because productivity comes to a standstill.

In order for **Empowerment** to succeed, you must conquer your fear. Seize the moment, and muster all your confidence to act. You have to face your fears in order to realize your true potential. The more you let fear dictate your actions, the less likely you will succeed in your career and in your life. Empower yourself to kick fear to the curb.

You Better Recognize! 10

Why should you care if you can help your company? No one pays attention.

Does it ever seem like no one notices when you do something well? This may be why some employees have reservations about using **Empowerment**. Recognition helps employees realize their worth to the company, and it unlocks their full potential.

Remember when you were a kid? You got excited when you received a good grade on a test or a report card. You worked hard for that grade and it paid off. You couldn't wait to bring home that piece of paper with the big red A+ on the front to show to your parents. You wanted your achievements to be acknowledged. You wanted the members of your family to appreciate the amount of blood, sweat, and tears that went into that A+. You were desperate to hear, *"Good job. **Keep up the great work**."* But what if you brought home your test, affixed it prominently to the fridge, and heard nothing for days and days? You would know that your parents see it because it's right there, but they still never mention it. Without that recognition or support from the people who are supposed to be on your side, you'd be unlikely to try as hard. Not surprisingly, next time your grades would suffer.

"There are two things people want more than sex and money -- recognition and praise."
Mary Kay Ash
American Businesswoman Founder of Mary Kay Cosmetics

For **empowerment** to work, and for employees to embrace their own talents and expertise and offer them up to their organizations, they need to be recognized. It's imperative that members of their team, the company, and their family acknowledge and appreciate their accomplishments and support their empowered decisions. The need for feedback is universal; everyone needs to be told when they are doing something well. The more your empowered decisions and achievements are recognized, valued, and respected, the more likely you are to use that creativity in the future on every project and with every problem.

For example, let's say you work at a call center with hundreds of employees and you take thousands of calls a week. You are required to limit all calls to less than 60 seconds. Customer service, creative thinking, and personal responsibility are subordinate to the clock. In a situation like this, what incentive would you have to make the empowered decision to solve an angry customer's problem, or over-deliver on a request? Let's say that, initially, you manage to consistently keep customers from dropping your service, but receive no positive reinforcement. You face quarterly performance reviews that hone in on deficiencies without mention of your successes. What's going to happen? Eventually, you will start feeling like your effort doesn't matter and that no one notices.

You will stop making empowered decisions, stop thinking outside the box. You'd eventually stop doing your best. Deciding to conserve the energy it takes to be truly effective, you stop going above and beyond to help your customers, co-workers, and the company, because *"what's the point?"* You will stop making yourself indispensable, because your team has made it clear that you are not.

Now, what if your manager routinely makes a habit of praising you for your hard work? What if she holds you up as an example to others for your empowered decision-making and your ability to increase customer retention? What if your company makes it clear that it values you as a significant contributor with employee incentive programs and recognition for success? How would that type of attitude and high level of managerial trust affect you on a daily basis? How would the company's obvious investment in you influence the support you receive from your team and, ultimately, the impact you are able to have on your organization on a daily basis? Wouldn't you be more likely to try to replicate your success? Wouldn't you be more likely to continue making the daring decisions rather than playing it safe?

It's this kind of recognition that feeds the **Empowerment** beast. You will keep making empowered decisions because you have been recognized for doing so.

"Praise is like sunlight to the human spirit: we cannot flower and grow without it."
Jess Lair, Ph.D.
American Educator, Author, and Advertising Director

"Praise, of all things, is the most powerful excitement to commendable actions, and animates us in our enterprises."
Jean de la Bruyere
French Essayist, and Moralist

I've Got the Power!

11

Nobody likes dealing with angry people or working through difficult situations. People can act irrationally. They can say hurtful and humiliating things. Problems can spiral out of control and leave everyone frustrated and looking for someone to blame. But, as an empowered employee, you thrive in nightmarish situations because they give you the opportunity to really show your stuff. You use all of your skills and experience to do what is possible to solve those problems. You bring order to anarchy to right the ship

The empowered employee can fix it.
Empowerment gives you the ability to use your talents and get creative! **Empowerment** is like having your own superpower that you can call on at any time.

You are the **EMPOWERED AVENGER,** and **Empowerment** is your secret weapon against chaos and hostility.

Now, every superhero needs an original story. Let's say you are a mild-mannered employee who goes to work every day at the electronics store and comes home every night, like most people. You're soft spoken at work and don't like to draw attention to yourself. You do your job well, but find yourself

Empowerment gives you the power to eliminate hostility every time.

Think of yourself as a superhero. You're the EMPOWERED AVENGER.

easily intimidated by hostile customers and avoid difficult situations whenever you can. In fact, you fear these types of problems and encounters. All you ever want to do is run away and hide.

One day, as you walk home, you somehow feel compelled to stop at a bookstore. Inside a mysterious force pulls you toward this very book, **Empowerment: A Way of Life**. You take a moment to imagine what a bit of **Empowerment** might do in your life. Not one to normally make impulse purchases, you decide to throw caution to the wind and buy the book.

Empowerment won't just change your job; it will change your life.

Armed with the new book, you get home and immediately feel the urge to read. You finish one chapter and quickly move on to the next. You start to feel differently, but you're not exactly sure how or why. As you finish the book, you fall asleep.

When you wake up the next morning, everything feels different. You pop right up out of bed with a newfound vigor, somehow ready to take on the world and eager to tackle any problem that crosses your path.

"He who is the most powerful has power over himself."
Seneca
Roman, Stoic, Philosopher, Statesman, and Dramatist

You get into work and suddenly you're more talkative. You have a newfound interest in your fellow employees and are curious about what they're working on that day. A customer, livid that a video game system she purchased doesn't work, is instantly transformed into an overhappy customer by your quick thinking and creative problem solving. You inject yourself into your co-workers' projects when they need help.

Tackling problems with a sense of purpose, you are committed to using your skills and talents to help yourself and the company succeed. Not quite sure where this feeling of responsibility and **Empowerment** has come from, you know it feels good, and you're hungry for more.

By turning to face the chaos rather than avoiding confrontation, you risk it all by putting your skills and your talents on the line. Not being afraid to speak up when you have an answer, you offer creative solutions to your company's biggest challenges. By embracing your unique qualities and displaying them proudly for all to see, a superstar is born. You are transformed. No challenge is too great. You have taken up the mantle of the Empowered Avenger!

Like every superhero, you have a nemesis: The Chaotic Situation. But as long as you accept your role and your responsibility, the Empowered Avenger can defeat the Chaotic Situation every time. **Empowerment** will make you feel like a superhero, because you'll be able to do things that you never could before. You will fight for your beliefs, take chances, and stop settling for mediocrity. You will soar in the face of adversity.

"The most common way people give up their power is by thinking they don't have any."
Alice Malsenior Walker
American Poet and Author of The Color Purple

EMPOWERMENT MAN'S NEMESIS: HOSTILE CUSTOMER

Let's Not Get Abusive | 12

Empowered employees accept the authority and responsibility to challenge established norms. They welcome the chance to think outside of their comfort zones in the name of productivity, efficiency, and success. Occasionally, good intentions go bad – the power to make decisions can be abused, knowingly or unknowingly.

After years of toiling under oppressive rules and burying their talents beneath fear and trepidation, newly empowered and liberated employees can sometimes find themselves going too far. No matter how skilled, talented, and well intentioned they are, some people might be tempted to shun their responsibilities, misuse their power, and abuse the trust placed in them. The temptation to take costly shortcuts, or make decisions based on personal gain, might be too great.

Empowerment is based on responsibility and trust, and the risks taken must support the established goals, the company's as well as your own.

For example, let's take a look at the game of baseball. There are clear sets of rules that guide the game. Most of the players follow the rules. Some obey them because they respect the history of the game. Others trust in their own physical

You will always find someone who will abuse the rules.

abilities and skills. Others stick to the rules because the officials enforce them to make sure they do. Despite these safeguards, some players choose to bend and break the rules to gain a minute statistical edge. Pitchers have been known to *"juice"* the ball to add a little extra movement to their curve. Batters drill holes in their bats and fill the inside with cork to make the ball jump off the barrel.

The worst offenders use performance-enhancing drugs such as steroids and HGH. Even when rules are altered and consequences change, players still continue to test the limits of the rules that exist.

"The abuse of a thing is no argument against the use of it."
Jeremy Collier
English Theatre Critic, non-juror Bishop and Theologian

No matter the consequences, be it professional or personal, you can always find someone willing to take advantage of the trust placed in them in an effort to stack the deck in their favor. Sometimes it works, sometimes it doesn't. Still, there will always be those select few who continue to cheat. You cannot control how other employees use their authority and responsibility as part of an empowered workforce, but you can control yourself. Sure, abuse happens, but the benefits of a truly empowered workforce far outweigh the potential for occasional abuse.

In the past, businesses feared **empowerment** because they focused on the small percentage of possibly negative outcomes. They did not look at the amount of creativity that was being lost because of that fear. Now, those same businesses have no choice. They are losing their best workers to the competition and falling behind in the global marketplace because they remain stuck in the past. For so long the tools to reinvent themselves were right in front of them: their employees. But they let fear of losing control-drive their decision-making rather than the desire to continuously develop, improve, and innovate.

Top management must endorse **Empowerment**. CEOs need to come out of hiding. They must embrace and promote an empowered workforce, not just give it lip service. For **Empowerment** to work there must be recognition and celebration. Keep in mind that almost all employees fear they will get fired for making empowered decisions, regardless of how much management supports it.

If your company is going to trust you enough to empower you, it has to trust that you will make decisions that benefit everyone. True **empowerment** does not exist unless your company allows its employees to utilize their own talents and experiences to circumvent rules and regulations when necessary, or make the difficult decision without looking for backup.

Abuse can occur. Frustration with an employer can create situations where workers feel exploited or neglected. They might feel entitled to more than they receive. By remaining an active participant in the projects and struggles of your co-workers, you can help quell those negative feelings and promote real teamwork. This approach not only yields tangible teambuilding results, it also provides a dramatically enhanced professional skill set.

The benefits of Empowerment far outweigh potential abuses.

Just as companies cannot focus on the small minority of employees who abuse **Empowerment**, you cannot concentrate on those negative situations either. You will run into customers and co-workers who might try to take advantage of you. They might try to get something for free, get you to do a job for them, or ask you to take responsibility for a mistake. Constantly fearing those situations will only paralyze you and lead to inaction. Approach all of your encounters with customers, co-workers, and supervisors with optimism. Keeping a positive attitude will allow you to be confident in your own abilities and to rely on the good intentions of the decisions you make.

It's much better for any company to promote **Empowerment** for their entire workforce and have some people go too far than to have a stagnant employee base. It's also dangerous to rely on top management to make all the decisions and hope they are correct.

You and your organization cannot constantly fear that abuse will take place.

What if customers get angry just so they can get something for free? So what! In reality, only 2 to 3 percent of customers will try to take advantage of you in this way. Most customers just want their problems solved – they're looking to you for answers. You are the expert; you have the knowledge and resources to make the necessary adjustments. You are the empowered employee.

What if a co-worker asks you for help with a project just so they can shirk their own responsibility? Who cares! Attack the project with the same enthusiasm you would any other. The point of **Empowerment** is that the cream will consistently rise to the top. Your employer empowered you for a reason. Your company wants you to reach and exceed your potential and it will be paying attention to how you perform. People will remember your outstanding work ethic and marvel at your ability to deliver creative solutions that produce unparalleled results.

If you and your organization constantly fear potential abuse, then you will not be able to exceed the personal and professional expectations you have for yourself. Don't get distracted with things that you cannot control and that ultimately have little to do with success or failure. A truly empowered workforce will make up for those losses a hundred fold. They will rise to the challenge and develop innovative solutions that will ensure growth and fuel future success.

If a company is only as good as its least empowered employee, why not empower them all?

You're Killing Me! 13

As mentioned, empowered employees can only reach and exceed their potential if they have the support of their company. The high level of trust your organization has placed in you can help overcome your fear, complacency, and apprehension. Likewise, your company can also stunt your development as a freethinking employee by micromanaging. Since the first business was created -- moving rocks up and down the Euphrates River -- there has been a micromanager looking over the shoulder of every laborer, ready to pass the blame, take credit, or offer a correction. It can be aggravating, insulting, and also completely counterproductive. It shreds **Empowerment** and tells workers that their employer does not trust them to make even the simplest of choices.

Just as employees have been systematically broken down over a period of decades, so too have managers grown accustomed to a certain status quo. Supervisors and management need to accept and embrace the individuality of their workers. In turn, employees are asked to respond to the needs of the company, fully utilizing their individual talents, skills and creativity, in order to transform their way of doing business.

Micro-management is an Empowerment killer.

"If you allow staff to own a project, you must trust in their capacity and avoid micro-management... Be there to provide support when needed but don't force yourself into the picture."
Barbara Moses
American Attorney

What does it mean to micromanage? The word *"micromanage"* is defined as *"to manage or control with excessive attention to minor details."*

Think about a real world example of micromanaging. You offer to help a co-worker with a time-sensitive project. A report is due that afternoon, and your colleague is struggling to format the data. Your boss is nervous, but you know what you need to do. At every step of the process your boss hovers over your shoulder, suggesting alternate methods and dispensing unsolicited advice. Sure, the guy means well, but he begins to get annoyed and wonder why you offered to help your co-worker. Micromanaging sucks the life out of your good-hearted offer to help. As a result, you might think twice before you agree to assist him in the future.

On the job, imagine that you are put in charge of a project. Your manager encourages you to take the reins. She makes it clear that she really wants to see what you can do. The empowered employee relishes this type of autonomy. Poised to dive in and to put your talents on display for the world to see, you can't wait to get started. As soon as you begin, your manager peppers you with questions about how you are handling inconsequential aspects of the project.

What are you doing? Why are you doing it like that? I would have done it another way. By constantly trying to check the power she has bestowed upon you, your manager has effectively sapped all of your **Empowerment**.

How can employees feel truly empowered while being micromanaged? **Empowerment** gives you control over your actions, decisions, and capabilities. The only way your company can get you to live up to those expectations and perform to the best of your abilities is to take off the training wheels and let you ride. Constantly questioning your every action and decision slows things down and introduces doubt into the process.

This returns you to a fearful state, where you are afraid to make your next move and are virtually paralyzed by fear. Employees who work under the pall of micromanagement are so afraid of their supervisors that they ease into routines to avoid getting noticed. Regardless of the chance for recognition, they settle for a bland and uneventful work life. Lacking **Empowerment**, their capacity for even the most basic creative thinking and problem solving is destroyed.

To combat a micromanaging manager, speak up. You will be the first to realize when it starts to affect the quality of your work, as well as your frustration level. Your manager may not even know that he is micromanaging you. You owe it to yourself to take responsibility for your performance.

Micro-management is Empowerment's worst enemy — its nemesis.

While it's uncomfortable, you'll have to take control of the situation and speak up. Explain how the constant advice and questioning affects your ability to do your job. Use this situation as an opportunity. Keep the dialogue open and discuss a variety of solutions. Be honest about your feelings and strive to create a relationship based on mutual respect and understanding. Now is the time to mention your previous successes. Be proactive and keep a list of times when you have reached or, better yet, exceeded goals. Talk about when you were given a job, allowed to work independently, and produced terrific results. Most of the time micromanagement is a result of disappointing work produced by other employees. Managers depend on workers to deliver and, when they don't, trust suffers. Appropriately voicing your concerns, presenting your successes, and restating the scope of the project can instill the mutual trust needed to get the job done while resolving the real issue.

Empower yourself to confront and address problems.

The empowered employee sees opportunities where others focus on problems. They meet challenges head on, soaring past the mediocre, bound for greatness. To reach such a vibrant and exciting goal, you're going to have to Empower yourself to confront others and address problems such as micromanagement when they occur.

What's In It For Me? 14

Like it or not, we live in a *"me"* world. Many people are only out for themselves, seeking the *"what's in it for me"* in every situation. They aren't going to make significant changes in the way they work or how they approach their personal development unless they see how it can benefit them directly.

Making customers happier is great for the company, but no matter how well intentioned and forward thinking, employees still need to know what's in it for them. Many people need to see concrete results. They want to chart their progress. Most importantly, they want to understand how the outcome benefits them and their world. Eager to experience the rewards for their labor, they usually want results sooner rather than later.

Empowered employees get results. They are rewarded with more frequent promotions because they have the platform to demonstrate their talents and skills. They are the movers and the shakers and are recognized by their customers, co-workers, and supervisors. Companies want to cultivate their own talent. They strive to hire from within. It is cheaper and more efficient than looking outside the organization. They are eager to promote internally and are constantly seeking empowered individuals

> *"Most people work just hard enough not to get fired and get paid just enough money not to quit."*
> George Carlin
> *American, five-time Grammy Award Winning Comedian, Social Critic, Actor, and Author*

who set examples for others to follow. Rising out of their midst as leaders, they motivate the masses to step up their games. Rather than waiting for a yearly performance review, an employee willing to take chances is more likely to get noticed.

Let's say you've been on the job for several years without a promotion. Your wages have stagnated. You feel like you haven't been given an opportunity to stand out. Let's face it, you probably haven't put yourself on the line or dared to put your talents on display either. You just expected your steady workflow and your mild-mannered temperament and seniority alone to move you up the chain of command. You see others pass you by. You might start to feel stuck and sorry for yourself. You think about this all the time, but all the thinking in the world isn't going to change your situation.

> *Somebody is going to be promoted. It might as well be you.*

You need action that is going to compel you to reach outside of your comfort zone. You need **Empowerment**. Go ahead, take on that risky project. Jump into a chaotic circumstance and clean up the mess. Use the skills and expertise you have built up over a lifetime to bring a new perspective to a tired and ineffective system. Others will take notice, and you will begin to fulfill your potential, but most importantly, you'll feel vibrant, alive and personally empowered. No longer content to watch others surpassing you, making more money, and getting promotions, you've become a dynamo. You charge ahead, making decisions, solving problems, and getting the results of your activities. You're Empowered.

Even if you do not immediately see monetary results, you will feel more satisfied with your performance. Your co-workers will angle to try to work with you. You'll look forward to taking on new and more complex responsibilities. You'll have more fun, stretching your creativity and building your skills. You'll be in control of your career and your life. Isn't that all anyone really wants? Personal power comes from doing the work you love and having it serve a purpose. Nothing is more fulfilling than knowing your efforts have made a mark on the world.

Tasks will be easier, projects will take less time, and you will be noticed for your increased productivity.

I Like Coming to Work!

Many employees don't go to work because they want to; they go because they have to. You spend 40 hours a week or more on the job. Most employees see their co-workers more than they see their own family or friends. Wouldn't you like to maximize your time? Don't you want to spend the majority of your week being as positive as possible?

Empowerment will help you create a more positive working environment.

Have you ever had a job you hated, one where everyone was constantly in a bad mood? Where no one trusted the organization or had any respect for the customers? How did you perform? How did you handle it? Negativity can be extremely contagious and create a miserable working environment. No one wants to be there. You find yourself dreading the thought of getting out of bed each day and keep hitting snooze on your alarm clock.

"It is not the employer who pays the wages. Employers only handle the money. It is the customer who pays the wages."

Henry Ford
American, Founder of Ford Motor Company

An empowered workforce creates a positive working environment that supports ingenuity, creativity, and innovation. Once you have the confidence and authority to trust your instincts and experiences, you can deal with anything that comes your way. Your work environment will become a more upbeat place. Your co-workers will help each other succeed. As contagious as negativity is, a positive vibe can be even more infectious. Then you might look forward to coming to work, making decisions that affect peoples lives and making them happy. Wouldn't it be terrific to enjoy those 40 hours each week rather than just suffering through them?

Companies like the previously mentioned Ritz-Carlton recognize employees for using **Empowerment**. Employee turnover at the Ritz is considerably lower than at other companies because its employees feel important and valued. Over the last few years, the Ritz has had an employee turnover rate in the teens compared to an average of between 40 and 60 percent for the rest of the hotel industry. This extraordinary statistic can only be achieved at a company where its employees are empowered to utilize their talents and creativity everyday. Empower yourself to be happy.

Making a Difference with Marketing | 15

Marketing is a blanket term that has come to mean just about anything. It can be defined as a host of professionals engaged in any number of activities that, hopefully, motivate a company's target market to respond favorably to a product or service. Often, budgets are large and results are hard to track. My overall advice would be to funnel some of the marketing money that is spent without measurable results into a powerful, relationship-building tool.

Funding **empowerment** seems to be a concept that would provide positive outcomes for employees and customers alike. Rather than thinking of this money as an extra, unbudgeted expense, why not consider it marketing money? Half the marketing money spent is wasted. Nobody knows which half is working and which half isn't.

You have a real customer, there in front of you, with a real or perceived problem. Through **empowerment,** you have options that would actually promote business. And isn't that the whole idea behind marketing in the first place? Utilizing a portion of a company's marketing budget to immediately solve problems and create overhappy customers who keep coming back seems to be a valuable use of any organization's money.

Marketing efforts are difficult to track and virtually impossible to measure. No one really knows what works and what doesn't. Even the most expensive campaigns fall flat and produce little or no real results. There are any number of reasons this can happen, and many things are beyond the control of the marketers. Plans are made using the best available information, and unforeseen things can happen to destroy even the best and most brilliant of campaigns.

But, when you have a customer right there in front of you with an issue, you should be in control. Often the options are spelled out for you, and all you really need is a bit of **Empowerment** to effectively market to the customer. I believe an employee's first and foremost reason for being is to keep the customer happy and coming back. This should always be the goal, and every possible resource should be available to make it happen.

I'm not sure where the misconception started that marketing efforts are exclusively focused on new customers. It's wrong and a big trap many companies fall into. Here's why.

- *Getting a new customer is 10 times more expensive than keeping one you already have.*

- *No matter how many new customers you are able to bring in, if more leave, you're on a crash course.*

- *Phenomenal marketing cannot make up for lackluster service.*

- *Happy customers are likely to make three referrals, while unhappy customers are likely to tell ten people. Those 10 people tell 10 others, who tell others, and before you know it, one unhappy client has done major damage.*

- *In the digital age, one unhappy customer can tell thousands of people in one post, blog, or email. There are now sites set up specifically to air complaints, and people use them before making purchasing decisions.*

Of course, marketing books are filled with loads of information like the preceding tips. Getting some additional knowledge would surely be beneficial, but it is important for me to say that I'm not promoting complex marketing techniques here. I am speaking about empowering employees to make rational, logical decisions in favor of the customer. These decisions, along with other sensible business practices, should go far in building a loyal customer base that positively impacts the bottom line on a consistent basis.

Here's a terrific example of marketing in action

Imagine a bank where employees are genuinely nice to you, call you by your name, and even open the door early for you. Think about a place where rules and regulations work in your favor, and employees are empowered to give you great service. At my bank, Star Choice Credit Union in Bloomington, Minnesota, they do just that.

Just the other day, I was sitting in the parking lot waiting for the bank to open, when an employee entered the parking lot. When I asked her what time the bank opens, Erin said, *"Mr. Tschohl, if you can wait a minute, I'll go in and I'll open the front door for you."* This is an example of **Empowerment** that cost Star Choice nothing but made an overhappy customer. She then helped me, as other employees arrived. One by one, as they came in, they greeted me, using my name. Scott Olson, the vice president, went to get me a cup of coffee, while I asked some questions about my recent statement. About 15 minutes later, the president, Dan Christiansen, stopped by to say, *"Hello,"* and went to refill my coffee cup.

I usually arrive about 8 a.m. and either Scott or Dan ALWAYS sees me drive up. One or the other opens the front door and invites me in.

At my previous bank, I can probably count on one hand the number of times anyone called me by my name in 20 years. Everyone knew me--they just never used my name. Nor would they ever open the doors even 10 seconds early. Now I am in heaven with a local bank that has mastered customer service and understands **Empowerment**.

Katie Grindeland, marketing manager, prepared the following information for me:

"In 2009, when the Executive Team announced we would be building a branch in Bloomington, MN, the Management Team knew we had to make an impact at that location right away. We could not be the financial institution that waited for everyone to come running in our doors. We had to be different. There had to be a reason people wanted to come in."

We knew one of those ways was with our service. We needed to break out from the credit union and bank mold and forge our own path. Without service distinction, our credit union would just be mundane. And we did not want to be mundane! We wanted people to hear about us, to learn about us through others' experience. We wanted to get word-of-mouth promotions about our service out into the community! So, we set out to improve our member (customer) service. While we always offered top-notch service, we knew that in our new location exceptional service could really make or break us. We can tell everyone how great we are, but if they come in and we can't walk the walk or talk the talk, we're in big trouble.

We educated all staff. From the president down to the member service representatives (tellers), everyone would need to know how to provide the best service possible. We wanted our community to receive the best service, no matter who they spoke to when they came in. We don't try to be like other financial institutions -- we do what works for us and what is best for the member. Below are just a few ways in which we try to be different:

1. *Customer satisfaction is always our main goal. Our employees are encouraged to bend the rules, when need be, in order to ensure customers are happy.*

2. *We try to always make the member's day—no matter what.*

3. *We listen. Whether it's about finances, their dog, their life, their job, we are a sounding board.*

4. *We do the little things: Open doors. Smile. Offer cookies. If it's raining, we offer umbrellas. The little things go a long way.*

5. *We are sincere. We want to help in any way we can.*

6. *We learn their story. We ask questions. We have conversations with members. We care about how their children are, how their kitchen remodel is going, how the graduation party went. We know a lot of our members on a first name basis—and they love that.*

7. *Every member is treated the same. Whether they have $1 or $100,000 in their account.*

8. *We open early and close late for members, if need be. We understand not all members are on the same schedule that we are. We want to make it a convenient place for them to bank.*

While we know we may be able to get an account by beating someone's rate or providing quick service, that's not helping build the relationship with the member. Our tagline—and our mission as an organization— is to build a strong financial future.

"We want to make sure we are doing everything we can to help our members get where they need to be financially. And with great service, it just makes it easier for them. They can trust us. We don't make them jump through giant hoops to get to where they want to be. They can trust us and rely on us to get them to where they need to be in one year, two years, even 10 years down the road. We made small changes that made a big difference. While we know that we can always and will always be improving, we are seeing the following benefits from our efforts.

- *Increased our new accounts by 430 percent from 2009 to 2010.*

- *Increased membership growth. Our new account growth is well above the national average for credit unions. The 2010 national average for credit unions is 1.0 percent, whereas Star Choice is 3.3 percent.*

- *Compared to 2009, our savings have increased an average of 19.15 percent. (National average 6.6 percent).*

- *Our loans have increased an average of 9.3 percent. (National average is -0.3 percent).*

- *Our assets have increased an average of 14.48 percent (National average is 4.7 percent).*

Most organizations are rule and policy driven. This stifles **Empowerment**. It costs nothing to open the doors early, smile, and address a customer by name. These are examples of **Empowerment** with NO cost--just great customer service.

Bend, Don't Break!   16

Every company has guidelines and processes to steer its employees. These standard operating procedures touch on many aspects of the business and cover a variety of potential situations that employees might face. It might seem like there is a rule for everything – one that stipulates how you are to perform during every minute of every day and under a wide variety of circumstances.

Companies that do not empower their workforce have extensive guidelines that mandate all sorts of mundane and common sense procedures. They pay statisticians and productivity experts millions of dollars to develop these processes, but they leave out the most important ingredient. Obviously absent from any manual is you or any mention of trust placed in you.

Companies that empower their employees want to cultivate the human element of their workforce. They realize that success hinges upon motivating and energizing a team. Guidelines at these companies are just that-guides. By not promoting hard and fast rules and processes that box in employees, they allow them to bring a level of personality to their job. They understand that too many rules stifle creativity and keep employees from reaching outside of themselves to be effective. While initially written to support employees in their efforts, companies that empower employees realize that strict adherence to any one policy will actually prevent the taking of risks that are necessary to succeed.

In addition, employees who work under stringent operating rules tend to hide behind them when the going gets tough. Rather than relying on their own expertise and ingenuity, they fall back on procedural processes that tell them what not to do rather than giving them the room to innovate.

The empowered employee has the authority and responsibility to bend any rule to the breaking point in order to serve a customer, over-deliver on a project, or utilize all available resources to solve a problem in a new and creative way.

Empowerment is all about bending the rules to keep the customer happy.

For example, you're heading up a project where a last-minute change comes in from a major client. Standard operating procedure tells you that you must get your supervisor to sign off on all changes before you can move forward, but that could bring the entire process to a standstill and delay delivery by several days. You are the project leader. You are the empowered employee. You have the necessary information and expertise. You know that the client won't be happy with the delay, so you make the decision to break that guideline and move forward in the name of efficiency.

Managers who support their employees' empowered decisions will understand the significance of the choice to move on rather than bring the entire endeavor to a screeching halt. Even if the change was technically incorrect, you made a decision based on the available information, weighing the pros and cons of seeking approval. The mix-up might give you the opportunity to revisit the approval process with your manager, but as an empowered employee, you made the correct decision. You should be recognized for your quick thinking and for bending the rules to create a winning situation for the organization and the customer.

The alternate narrative saps you of your power to use your common sense and talent to bridge the divide between the guideline and reality. You don't want to risk getting in trouble. You are unsure of your own feelings and instincts regarding the project and the client. You know the procedure, so you decide to march in step with it. You decide to pass along the change for approval, the project shuts down in the meantime, and the client rages. You might feel bad for a minute, but the procedure holds up your decision as valid, regardless of the negative outcome. The rule remains as strong as ever even though you, your client, your co-workers, and the organization suffer because you ignore your chance to be extraordinary.

Bending the rules in the name of productivity and efficiency creates a winning situation for everyone.

"Rules aren't necessarily sacred, principles are."
Franklin D. Roosevelt
32nd President of the United States

Rules and guidelines that do not support **Empowerment** must be thrown out or changed. Empower yourself to take the reins when your company updates its standard operating procedures. Look for ways to improve existing policies to create space in which employees can maneuver rather than caging them in. You owe it to yourself and your company to throw away outdated procedures and complex processes.

Companies and employees need to be nimble. They must be swift enough to adapt to the changing economic landscape. Empowered decision makers have a responsibility to look for inconsistencies in company guidelines that mitigate or completely negate opportunities for creativity, innovation, and reinvention. Companies need to put employees first when they design their rules and regulations and work backward to allow a little room to breathe, daydream, imagine, learn, and grow.

Empower yourself to bend the rules to the breaking point when necessary.

The Need For Speed! 17

You can empower yourself. You can become the most valued person in your organization. But there's more.

Have you ever heard the expression, ***"it pays to be quick?"*** Consider this example: A customer approaches you while you are wrapping a package for shipment. She asks you to refund her purchase, but she doesn't have a sales receipt. Do you put her off until your manager returns, or do you resolve the problem for her?

Given what you've read so far in this book, your choice should be easy. But there's one thing to complicate your action: Your boss wants you to finish wrapping that package, and you've yet to take inventory, which you also need to complete by closing.

You turn to your customer ***"Yes, I can refund that for you"***. Good decision. But then you add, ***"I need to finish wrapping this package first. Can you give me a moment please?"*** Then you walk away to get the packing tape, so you can finish that job.

Now you're almost finished, but your customer has waited almost five minutes. As she has watched you finish a wrapping, the message to her is that a package is more important than her business. You give her the refund. She turns gruffly and walks away.

So what does this have to do with Empowerment? Everything.

You made an empowered decision, but it took so long to deliver on it that you still lost your customer.

Without **Empowerment**, you'll always experience delays, but when you make an empowered decision, you must move quickly to act upon your decision.

Fast, empowered decisions help you reach your goal.

Empowerment means making fast decisions. The longer it takes you to decide, the more agitated the customer will become. Whether customer, co-worker or supervisor, everyone wants to be heard and responded to. Customers want service; they want their problems solved right away, without any obstacles or red tape. Your goal is to move them through your business as quickly as possible. Your speed contributes to their satisfaction. If you have to ask three different people for permission to act, then you're at a standstill.

Empowerment gives you the permission to speed things up. It places the decision in your hands.

We know what it means to make quick decisions. Consider the impact on both sides of an interaction. A customer accidentally leaves her ID card on the counter after checkout.

Your company policy requires that all lost property goes into a safe. The customer returns, asking if anyone has found an ID. You say that you will gladly check for her and then find her ID in the safe. Now imagine yourself as the customer. You're anxious because you've misplaced your ID. Will you have to replace it? Is your identity exposed to potential fraud? You ask an employee to search for your ID; the longer you wait, the more your tension mounts. But the employee returns right away with your ID. You exhale. What would have happened if the employee were not empowered to open the safe? If the employee did not move swiftly, you can only imagine…

Speed and **Empowerment** go hand in hand. Think of speed as the jelly to **Empowerment**'s peanut butter. They form a perfect combination.

"I'm so fast, last night I turned off the light switch in my hotel room and was in bed before the room was dark."
Muhammad Ali
American Boxer and threetime World Heavyweight Champion

Speed and Empowerment go hand in hand.

Is It Something I Said?

18

It's happened to all of us. At some point in our lives, we've said the wrong thing at the wrong time. It could be a simple comment you made to your significant other, one that was misinterpreted. Or something you said to a friend that was twisted into an argument. Any way you slice it, what you say and how you say it can cause a conflict.

Sometimes the simplest words can define your interaction. The smooth talker uses the right words to calm an irate customer. An agitator uses words that trigger conflict. We're not born as smooth talkers. It's a skill acquired to ensure safe and satisfactory encounters.

A couple of phrases that will go a long way toward positive interaction are the obvious ones: *"please"* and *"thank you"*. You would be surprised at how effective these two simple phrases are. Customers want to feel important, to be valued, and to be treated with respect. It's a choice you make that produces big results. Consider your options: You have to place a customer on hold. You could say, *"Hold on a second"*, or *"Could you please hold?"* Then you could return to the call with, *"What were we talking about"*, or *"Thank you for your patience."*

"A word uttered cannot be taken back."
African Proverb

"Words are also actions, and actions are a kind of words."
Ralph Waldo Emerson
American Poet, and Philosopher

"By swallowing evil words unsaid, no one has ever harmed his stomach."
Winston Churchill Emerson
British Prime Minister, Noted Statesman, and Orator

Here are some other phrases to avoid and words that should be used instead:

Phrases to Avoid	Instead Use:
You have to call this number for that	We can fix your problem
I'll try to fix it.	I will fix it.
It's not our policy.	Let's figure how we can take care of this.
You should have read the warranty.	Are you familiar with the warranty on this item?
I can't help you.	Let me see what I can do.
What did you say?	I'm sorry, it's really loud in here, could please repeat that?
No.	I will look into that.
Hang on a second...	Could you hold on for just one second?
That's not my job.	I'm happy to take care of this for you.
What do you want?	How can I help you?

"The difference between the right word and the almost right word is the difference between the lightning and a lightning bug."
Mark Twain
American Humorist, Author of Adventures of Huckleberry Finn.

Empowerment is often about choices. Empower yourself to use the correct words when talking to customers. You will be amazed at the difference it will make.

Maxing it Out 19

Peer influence is increasingly more important to productivity. Previously, employees relied on top brass, managers, and supervisors for leadership. Today's workforce looks to natural leaders in their peer group. Supporting **Empowerment** increases the positive influence these leaders have within their employee ranks.

There's at least one in every company. They're the ones with their fingers on the industry's pulse. They see the big picture. They know what's going on at their company and behind the doors at the competition. Highly skilled, they're experts at their jobs. They're not just good at what they do; they can also offer helpful suggestions to others. You can easily spot them; they're who everyone goes to when there's a problem. They're the real power of their organizations and, if you empower them, you empower your workforce.

Take a minute and think about harnessing their influence. These leaders can help you make great strides in delivering the message of **Empowerment**. They might have more of their co-worker's trust than management. Utilizing them as a valuable resource could fuel the efforts to promote **Empowerment**.

"Leadership is influence."
John C. Maxwell
American Author, Speaker, and Pastor

> *"Effective leadership is not about making speeches or being liked; leadership is defined by results not attributes."*
>
> Peter Drucker
> *Austrian Author, Professor, and Management Consultant*

A win-win would be to have them participate in all aspects of the entire initiative.

People are motivated to work harder when they are part of the decision. When someone takes ownership, they are more personally invested in the outcome. Encouraging those natural leaders to more fully participate actually increases a company's employee return on investment.

Let's face it, you can't be everywhere. By having these employee leaders on board with the concept of **Empowerment**, you'll have built- in cheerleaders coaching, promoting, and propelling your efforts forward. What could be better than minimum resources producing maximum results? Now that's leadership.

Bridging the Gap | 20

Every organization in every industry has high-value customers. These are the people with powerful titles, positions of influence, substantially increased purchasing power, or a combination of these qualities. Statistically, they deliver anywhere from 80 percent of a company's revenue while representing 20 percent of the client base. High-value customers either spend large amounts of money when they purchase, or buy small quantities on such a regular basis that they have a significant impact on the bottom line. They're not the regular clients whose business seemingly goes unnoticed. These people have real buying power. With them, the dollar swing is larger; if they move, a company will feel it.

High-value customers receive better treatment. They enjoy the rewards of their status, including name recognition, immediate and expanded service, and increased privileges. They're treated differently, and it's in a company's best interest to do so.

Employees are encouraged to be empowered to break any rules or regulations to keep high-value customers happy. Moving a problem up the ladder, or stalling service to someone of this status, could have devastating and long-term negative effects.

Loyalty programs are used in virtually every customer-driven industry. Rewards vary, depending on the level of consumption, frequency of use, and dollars spent. Status increases with additional purchases, psychologically tapping the human desire for recognition, power, and achievement. These programs offer a wealth of targeted information and personalized data that reveal individual spending patterns. At the most basic level, they are used to immediately alert employees concerning the customer's purchasing habits. These programs use fancy names, distinct colors, or numerical codes to differentiate status levels. These categories make it easy for employees to know how much **Empowerment** to use when dealing with these customers.

I am a Diamond Medallion traveler with Delta Airlines. To earn this grade, I have to fly at least 125,000 miles per year. With Diamond status, which is currently the highest echelon Delta has, I am entitled to a host of amenities, including three free pieces of checked baggage weighing up to 70 pounds each, unlimited upgrades, and complimentary membership in Delta Sky Club.

I enjoy these perks, but the one I really value is the high level of customer service I receive. In reality, I am never more than a phone call away from solving any problem. They are willing to do more for me because they have to. My purchasing power is significant because of my level of flying. If they treated everyone like they treat me, they would own the market. Making everyone feel like royalty would produce overhappy customers eagerly awaiting their next flight.

People at this level of flying are constantly being romanced by the other airlines. Amenities have become increasingly more important as airlines lobby to lure these high revenue fliers away from their current loyalty programs.

As a businessman, I understand the game: you give more to get more. But, the customer service expert in me looks a little deeper.

I'm curious about what would happen to an airline that bucked the bare bones approach and treated their customers like kings and queens. Imagine a company leading the charge toward improved service. Think about the impact empowered employees could have on the bottom line by bending the rules in favor of the customer.

Keep Them Coming Back | 21

Plain and simple, when you're empowered, people want to work with you. Whether in business or outside the workplace, don't we all want people to seek us out because they like to work with us? In business, your goal is to keep people coming back, again and again. The only way to do this is to make sure your customers are overhappy.

You don't want people to take their business elsewhere. You don't want people to avoid you because you can't make a decision. Why would they, if they are elated with the service that you provide them?

It's natural. We like things to be easy. You want your company to be the first one people think of when they have a need that requires the services or products you provide. When you used **empowerment** to make them happy the last time, you made sure they were going to come to your business the next time. A while back, I was at Outback Steakhouse, and my steak was just not very good. I asked the server to replace it, and she immediately said she would. I was surprised at how quickly she made the decision. Then she said, *"To make up for the inconvenience I'd like to buy each of you a free dessert"*.

"We see our customers as invited guests to a party, and we are the hosts. It's our job every day to make every important aspect of the customer experience a little bit better."
Jeff Bezos
American, CEO, Amazon.com

She proceeded to bring over the manager with free desserts for everyone. The manager supported her in her empowered decision. She went out of her way to ensure that she had an entire group of overhappy customers.

Let's look at this more closely. The retail cost of the dessert was $5 each but the cost of goods was probably only about $1 each. Most important is the fact that she took control of a potentially negative situation and created positive results. This is a great example of both service recovery and **Empowerment**. She got an excellent tip because of her great service.

Empowerment helps your retain customers.

I've used this example in some of my speeches and have written about this in my free service newsletter (go to **www.customer-service. com** to subscribe) that goes out to thousands of people throughout the world. For an investment of $3, Outback Steakhouse has gotten thousands of dollars in advertising and a loyal customer. I go to Outback once a month.

So, how do you retain customers and make people want to work with you? **Empowerment**, that's how! **Empowerment** allows you to guarantee that your customers have a positive experience every time so they keep coming back, time after time after time.

Surprise!

It's Valentine's Day. You've bought your wife
flowers and chocolates. She expects them, and
you deliver. It's a nice gesture, but there is very
little surprise involved. Guys, you know if you
don't get her something on Valentine's Day you're
in the doghouse and probably will get to sleep
on a very special surface that night: the couch.
Ladies, you feel if he doesn't get you something
on this day, then he doesn't care. However, have
you ever bought flowers for your girl for no
special reason? Chances are, she didn't expect
them and was pleasantly surprised. Customers
want that attention too – not the flowers, just the
knowledge that you want them to be overhappy.

Most customers who walk into a business with a
problem are in a hurry. Time is money – you can
read it on their faces and sense their impatience. It's
natural to be offended by customers who express
that impatience through rudeness. Many people
are conditioned to think that you won't be able
to do anything to help them. They have negative
expectations. This is your chance to surprise them.
If you make them happy in a timely manner,
you will greatly exceed their expectations and no
doubt improve their mood. Your goal is to astonish
and amaze them with your level of service.

*Customers
want to be
surprised.*

"Again, your challenge is not just to improve. It is to break the service paradigm in your industry or market so that customers aren't just satisfied, they're so shocked that they tell strangers on the street how good you are."

Jack Welch

American Businessman, Author., Former Chairman and CEO of General Electric

Let's say a customer comes into a bank distraught because she accidentally left her ATM card in the machine. She says that she needs to order another card and she knows that it will take a few days. She's says it's unfortunate, because she used it as a debit card, too, but she understands it will take a little time for the card to arrive in the mail. You inform her that you can issue her a temporary card right away. Watch the frown turn into a grin and the tension rise into the clouds. The customer is excited and happy that she will have a card to use immediately. With one simple action, you have exceeded her expectations. By surprising her, you have ensured that she will continue to do business with your bank and will look for you on future visits.

Empower yourself to surprise your customers. And watch them come back again and again.

Take My Word for It | 22

Your mother used to tell you that sticks
and stones break bones – but there are
times when words can harm you.

Last week, you saw a preview for a movie that
looked like it was right up your alley. You and your
friend decide to go check out a matinee. But the
movie was a huge letdown – it stunk. You wasted
your time and money, and you want to make sure
no one falls into the trap that snared you. While
having drinks with your friends the next day, you
tell them all about your terrible cinema experience.
They tell all their friends, and soon the rumor
wagon is on the move; this film is a stinker. The
film does poorly at the box office. OK, it wasn't
your doing, but many others probably shared
your feelings – with as many of their friends.

Often, failure is directly related to bad word
of mouth. When something's bad, people tell
others. And those people tell others. Studies
show that out of 100 dissatisfied customers,
a business tends to lose 32-36 existing or
potential customers. That's just the way it is.

Bad word of mouth can sink your business.

Bad word of mouth can sink your business faster than that iceberg sank the Titanic. The last thing you want is someone having a bad experience with your business or to point a finger at you, because the bad experience will be just the start of a downhill flow of problems. The word spreads. Before you know it, you're not retaining customers, you're losing them. When businesses lose customers, they lose money. Sooner or later, if your company loses enough customers, it will go out of business. When it goes out of business, your job will be gone. You MUST create a positive experience for your customers, because the opposite can be devastating for you and your company.

Happiness is Contagious!

You must create a positive experience for your customers.

You've got an emergency. A water pipe has just burst in your house, and water is running everywhere. Your house is like a water park without the fun. You need to fix this problem as soon as possible, before your house is lost like the city of Atlantis. Find a plumber – one that reacts quickly. However, you've never needed a plumber before and have no idea who to call. You could look someone up on the Internet, but anyone can list there, and how do you know if they are any good? So, what do you do? You call your friend and ask him if he knows a good plumber. Your friend says that, in fact, he does; there's a guy he had come out last year and he did a great job. He gives you the plumber's number, you call, and your problem is fixed without any further damage.

Your friend had a positive experience with this particular plumber and shared it with you, giving the plumber more work and a new customer. This was all due to positive word of mouth.

You can now see the additional benefits of overhappy customers. They will share their positive experiences with others, generating positive word of mouth about your company. You want your customers saying to their friends, ***"I had such a great experience at this company. I will go back. You should go there."*** People like to talk; people like to gossip. They will talk about their experiences with your business. You want to make sure that, when they open their mouths, they have nothing but good things to say about your organization.

Some of the most successful companies in the world have been built through positive word of mouth. All of the best companies in the world have been built on great service. It's a fact that, when people get treated well, they are happy and want everyone to know about it. Word of mouth is the cheapest, most effective, and least time-consuming method of marketing there is. The concept is simple and easy to produce: just create overhappy customers. Companies that take care of their customers get new customers. Due to its low cost and high impact, word of mouth is essential to your business. Empowered employees will go a long way toward making that happen.

Some of the most successful companies in the world have been built through positive word of mouth.

The Rules of Empowerment: Wait, You Mean There are Limits?

23

Empowerment does mean taking on additional roles and responsibilities. However, no one is giving you the keys to the kingdom. All power has limits and, for **Empowerment** to succeed, clear parameters need to be defined.

So, what's a parameter? A parameter is basically a boundary or a restriction. For example, at the airport, you can't bring anything you want on the plane. There are certain parameters that indicate what you can carry on, and what gets left behind. You're not empowered if you extend beyond the parameters. You're probably arrested.

> *"The difference between genius and stupidity is that genius has limits."*
>
> Albert Einstein
> *German Theoretical Physicist, Philosopher, and Author*

Wait Until I Tell My Friends About This!

Right now some of you might feel like you've been given complete freedom, and you can do whatever you want. However, being empowered does not give you the authority to create your own dictatorship where you get to call all the shots. **Empowerment** gives you permission to appease angry customers with a refund, gift certificate, or merchandise. It does not grant permission to give away a bunch of free stuff to family and friends. That is not **empowerment**. There's a more technical term for that. It's called stealing!

I'm Going to be Rich!

> *Directly profiting from a customer is stealing.*

While some of you might be rich someday, being empowered does not give you the authority to use customers as a source of personal profit. You will profit from **empowerment**, but indirectly, not directly. What's the difference?

Let's say your company has a 30 day return policy. A customer comes in with an item that's broken. However, he purchased it nearly a year ago, obviously way beyond the return policy time limit. The item cost him nearly $200, and he's not happy at all about the fact that it's broken.

But this clever customer has an idea. If he slips you $20, could you "look the other way and allow his return?" Then you could be really clever and gladly accept the money as you process his return. Again, this is directly profiting from a customer. While you might like to think of it as **empowerment**, it's actually just stealing.

Empowerment lets you profit indirectly

Think about the same scenario. Only this time, you tell the customer you are very sorry that he is past the return window, but because he is such a valuable customer, you are happy to give a 25 percent off coupon on his next purchase. Odds are very good that he will take that coupon and use it to buy a new item. In his mind, not using that coupon is like throwing money away. So, he purchases a new item, which means a direct profit for the company and an indirect profit for you. What is your indirect profit? Your manager will take note of how well you handled the customer, which greatly increases the odds of a raise or promotion in your future.

Empowerment allows you to profit indirectly, not directly.

Say When...

Did you ever hear the expression, *"There is a time and place for everything?"* The same can be said about **Empowerment**. Over time, you will learn the right times and places for utilizing **Empowerment**. Until then, follow this principle: Use **Empowerment** with any problems, issues, or difficult encounters that necessitate a quick decision.

Let's say you're ringing up a sale for a nice, elderly lady. She is an unusually pleasant customer. She asks you how your day is going and actually appears to be genuinely interested in your response. You smile at her and return her kind words. She seems like a nice person, so you give her a $10 off coupon. Seems like a perfect opportunity to use **Empowerment**, right?

Wrong! This customer is not irate or upset. In fact, she appears to be the opposite, exceptionally happy and cheerful. What fire are you trying to put out by giving her a coupon? She will come back as long as you are pleasant and friendly to her. There is no need to try to make her overhappy, because she's already walking on sunshine.

It's imperative that you learn the correct times and places to use Empowerment.

Empowered workers set themselves up to succeed in any environment. They can shine anywhere, because they are quick, agile, and proactive. Not satisfied to sit on the sidelines, they aggressively lead the charge. They show up at work each day with knowledge in abundance, a lifetime of learning, and a desire to challenge the status quo. They see their work as important and continually strive to increase the value of their efforts. Not comfortable looking to others for solutions, they move forward, making decisions that impact the lives of others.

They seek opportunities to use their newly found power and don't just rely on it when they are in difficult situations. **Empowerment** is limited only by their creativity and desire to propel themselves and their company forward. Workers who practice empowered behavior on a regular basis are more able to maximize it when dealing with an irate customer, or when an immediate solution is needed to address a challenging problem. As with everything else, practice makes perfect.

It's imperative that you learn the correct times and places to use **empowerment**. Understanding these limits will ensure everyone's success.

Everyone Likes A Winner!

24

Ever been in a situation where you feel like you can't win? For example, let's say you and a friend get into an argument. You each have an opinion, and you both feel that you are right. Neither one of you wants to back down, and you continue to argue. It escalates until the friendship as a whole is affected. The end result is that you're no longer friends. Now, neither one of you is happy, because you've both lost a friend. This is what's known as a lose-lose situation. No one ends up happy, and this situation must be avoided at all costs.

A lose-lose situation for your company would be when an angry customer comes in and you can't do anything to help him. He leaves the organization angry, and now you're in a bad mood because you just had to deal with an irate customer and felt powerless. Nobody's happy. Your organization never wants a lose-lose situation. Think of the typical irate customer who comes in. You have many different ways you can respond to her. Remember, however, the underpowered response will lead to a lose-lose situation.

A lose-lose situation must be avoided at all costs.

Now think of the above example again. What if both friends had decided to concede that the other one has a point? They would both realize that their friendship is too valuable to be broken up by one petty argument. This is what's known as a win-win situation. Both parties get what they want: they get to feel like they are right and they get to keep a friend.

Empowerment Can Make YOU a Winner!

Empowerment is a win-win situation.

Empowerment is a win-win situation. Both you and your customers are satisfied. Customers have their problems solved quickly; you learn the skills needed to diffuse a difficult situation so that you retain them as customers. More importantly, **Empowerment** is the way to gain control of your work and your life.

- *To step up and be accountable.*

- *To gain the authority and permission to satisfy customers.*

- *To accelerate your path to professional and personal development.*

Empowerment always leads to a win-win situation. This book has helped you learn the skills and the traits of an empowered person. Focus on making quick decisions.

You have to make the choice. Get to know your business. Take the authority and permission granted by your employer – to serve customers.

Some of the concepts in this book might seem revolutionary. The strategies outlined here address a host of challenges that must be overcome at every level in every organization. As the world becomes a smaller place with even the most basic transactions being conducted on a global level, the need for quick and personal service is even more important. As anyone who's spent hours on the phone with someone outsourced to India can tell you, it's not the easiest possible way to get a problem solved. The powerlessness felt could easily be avoided by having someone, physically there, to help you.

As I travel the world I am astounded at the lack of **Empowerment**. This is only surpassed by the myth that executives have about their level of employee **Empowerment**. Top leaders honestly believe their employees are empowered, and that couldn't be further from the truth. The chance of them making an empowered decision is as high as the likelihood of them running a marathon. They need support, recognition, and lots of training on **Empowerment**. You'll never be a service leader without **Empowerment**.

In this book I have tried to make a strong case for **Empowerment** as a strategy for both employee and organizational success. It is my hope that these strategies are embraced and through them policies and procedures are adjusted to support **Empowerment**. Focused attention and the necessary resources should be given to achieving the highest level of **Empowerment**. If you take away only one thing from this book, I hope it is the knowledge that any organization is only as strong as its least empowered employee. My message to you is loud and clear: success is contingent on **Empowerment**!

I sincerely hope you have enjoyed this book and that for you **Empowerment** will become A Way of Life.

And finally, I encourage you to read my other books on customer service to help you develop a service strategy and to improve your own performance. I have been reading at least one self-improvement book per month for the last 40 years. Some are better than others. These books, listed on the last page, give me leading-edge ideas and keep me highly motivated. One of the best investments you can make is in yourself.

If you have thoughts, comments, or ideas about this book,
I'd love to hear from you. Feel free to write or call me.

John Tschohl
Service Quality Institute
9201 East Bloomington Freeway
Minneapolis, Minnesota 55420-3497 USA
952-884-3311 fax 952-884-8901
Email: quality@servicequality.com
Web-site: www.customer-service.com
Web-site: www.EmpowermentAWayofLife.com
Facebook®: www.facebook.com/johntschohl
Twitter®: twitter.com/johntschohl
Linked in®: http: www.linkedin.com/in/johntschohl

Service Quality Institute provides a variety of customer service
programs that can help your organization create a service culture
and develop high performing employees. Our products change
behaviors and attitudes and teach the art and skills of customer
service while building employee morale and facilitating teamwork.
All of our programs are based on achieving awesome service
through recognition. In addition to this book, Service Quality
Institute offers a structured training program, **Empowerment:
A Way of Life,** that you can use to train your total workforce.

If you are interested in learning more about Service Quality Institute's
training programs or about John Tschohl's seminars and speeches,
please contact Service Quality Institute at the above address.

ALSO BY
JOHN TSCHOHL

ACHIEVING EXCELLENCE THROUGH
CUSTOMER SERVICE
(Best Sellers Publishing, 2008,
ISBN: 0-9636268-4-4, $19.95)

LOYAL FOR LIFE
(Best Sellers Publishing, 2005,
ISBN: 0-9636268-8-4, $14.95)

E-SERVICE
(Best Sellers Publishing, 2001,
ISBN: 0-9636268-6-8, $24.95)

CA$HING IN
(Best Sellers Publishing, 1995,
ISBN: 0-9636268-2-5, $14.95)

THE CUSTOMER IS BOSS
(Best Sellers Publishing, 1993,
ISBN: 0-9636268-0-9, $19.95)

These books and additional copies of **Empowerment: A Way
of Life** are available in local bookstores. For volume orders,
contact Best Sellers Publishing at 952-888-7672 or by e-mail.
If you want an empowered workforce, you should introduce
a new training program on customer service at least every
four to six months. There is no magic bullet or book that will
change an individual's life. Repetition and reinforcement are
critical to getting your entire staff to be customer driven.

For more information to offer comments or ask questions,
please email us at **BSP@BestSellersPublishing.com**